Physical Characteristics of the Greater Swiss Mountain Dog
(from the American Kennel Club)

Body: Full with slight tuck up. The loins are broad and strong. The croup is long, broad and smoothly rounded to the tail insertion.

Topline: Level from the withers to the croup.

Tail: Thick from root to tip, tapering slightly at the tip, reaching to the hocks and carried down in repose. The bones of the tail should feel straight.

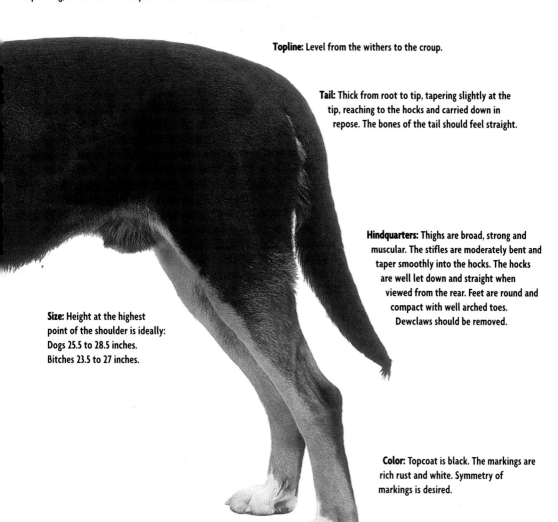

Hindquarters: Thighs are broad, strong and muscular. The stifles are moderately bent and taper smoothly into the hocks. The hocks are well let down and straight when viewed from the rear. Feet are round and compact with well arched toes. Dewclaws should be removed.

Size: Height at the highest point of the shoulder is ideally: Dogs 25.5 to 28.5 inches. Bitches 23.5 to 27 inches.

Color: Topcoat is black. The markings are rich rust and white. Symmetry of markings is desired.

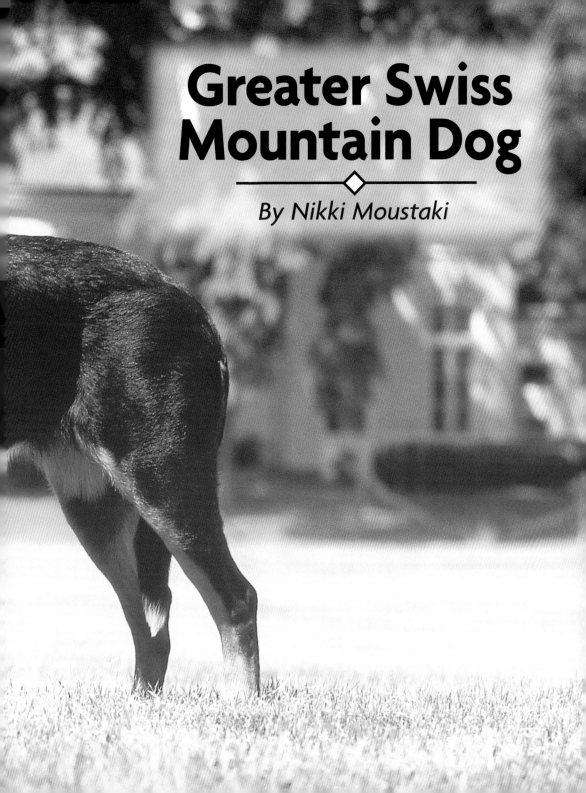

Greater Swiss Mountain Dog

By Nikki Moustaki

Contents

Training Your Greater Swiss Mountain Dog **80**

Begin with the basics of training the puppy and adult dog. Learn the principles of house-training the Greater Swiss Mountain Dog, including the use of crates and basic scent instincts. Enter puppy kindergarten, introduce the pup to his collar and leash and progress to the basic commands. Find out about obedience classes and other activities.

Healthcare of Your Greater Swiss Mountain Dog **101**

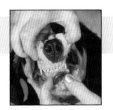

By Lowell Ackerman DVM, DACVD
Become your dog's healthcare advocate and a well-educated canine keeper. Select a skilled and able veterinarian. Discuss pet insurance, vaccinations and infectious diseases, the neuter/spay decision and a sensible, effective plan for parasite control, including fleas, ticks and worms.

Your Senior Greater Swiss Mountain Dog **130**

Know when to consider your Greater Swiss Mountain Dog a senior and what special needs he will have. Learn to recognize the signs of aging in terms of physical and behavioral traits and what your vet can do to optimize your dog's golden years. Consider some advice about saying goodbye to your beloved pet.

Showing Your Greater Swiss Mountain Dog **141**

Step into the center ring and find out about the world of showing pure-bred dogs. Here's how to get started in AKC shows, how they are organized and what's required for your dog to become a champion. Take a leap into the realms of obedience trials, agility trials, tracking tests and more.

KENNEL CLUB BOOKS® GREATER SWISS MOUNTAIN DOG
ISBN: 1-59378-375-2

Copyright © 2007 • Kennel Club Books® • A Division of BowTie, Inc.
40 Main Street, Freehold, NJ 07728 USA
Cover Design Patented: US 6,435,559 B2 • Printed in South Korea

Library of Congress Cataloging-in-Publication Data
Moustaki, Nikki, 1970-
Greater Swiss mountain dog / by Nikki Moustaki.
p. cm.
ISBN 1-59378-375-2
1. Greater Swiss mountain dog. I. Title.
SF429.G78M68 2006
636.73--dc22   2006011614

10 9 8 7 6 5 4 3 2

Photography by Isabelle Français
with additional photographs by:

Ashbey Photography, Paulette Braun, Bernd Brinkmann, Carolina Biological Supply, Tara Darling, JC Photography, Carol Ann Johnson, Bill Jonas, Dr. Dennis Kunkel, Tam C. Nguyen, Phototake, Kenneth Reed Photography, Jean Claude Revy, The Standard Image and Alice van Kempen.

Illustrations by Patricia Peters

The publisher wishes to thank all of the owners whose dogs are illustrated in this book.

The Swissy has arrived! Although still considered a rare breed, the Greater Swiss Mountain Dog is a versatile working dog and an excellent companion dog, a combination that won't let the breed remain rare for long.

GREATER SWISS MOUNTAIN DOG

The Greater Swiss Mountain Dog (GSMD) is known for his dedication to his owners and property and his strong body and diligent work ethic that make him an excellent draft dog. The "Swissy" is one of four breeds that make up a group called the Swiss *Sennenhunden*; the others are the Entelbucher, the Appenzeller and the Bernese Mountain Dog. The GSMD has an unusual and long history, being one of the oldest breeds from Switzerland yet a relative newcomer to the American pure-bred dog fancy.

Unfortunately, the history of the Swissy is something left up to the suspicions of historians to a great extent. Although there are no official records, the history of the breed presumably begins over 2,000 years ago. Most people believe that the Swissy is derived from the Molosser, a breed that was brought into the region now known as Switzerland when the Romans occupied the area in about 100 BC. No one knows much about the dogs already in Switzerland at that time, but it is presumed that the Roman dogs bred with the native dogs, and the forerunner of the GSMD eventually emerged.

There is another theory that dogs owned by the Phoenicians who inhabited Spain around 1100 BC started to spread across Europe and also contributed to the origins of the Swissy's bloodline, but no one knows for certain. Historians do know that the Swissy is a

The Entelbucher (RIGHT) and the Appenzeller (BOTTOM) are two of the Sennenhund breeds and are related to the Greater Swiss Mountain Dog.

forefather of both the Saint Bernard and the Rottweiler.

Around the time of the GSMD's appearance, dogs were bred for work (as they still are today). Farmers mated together dogs with the ability to perform similar tasks, creating offspring that were also good at that particular chore. This is how the Swissy's propensity for pulling carts or sleds was established. Swissys were used for other farm-related chores, like guarding and herding. The breed was also used as a butcher's dog and worked a great deal with livestock on cattle farms. The Swissy is known as a "generalist," as he is able to perform many tasks but, because of this, he can lose focus easily.

As the Swissy was bred more and more for draft work, this became the breed's specialty. It was still used for other purposes, but physically the Swissy was gaining the muscular back legs and solid physique required for drafting.

The drafting quality of the Swissy made it an excellent resource for farmers. The Swissy could also be used for human

By combining the desirable traits of certain dogs, farmers were able to create a breed that was beneficial in the field. The result was the exceptionally well-built, loyal and loving Greater Swiss Mountain Dog.

Though a rare breed, the Greater Swiss Mountain Dog can be found on the international dog-show circuit; this attractive Swissy competes at the World Dog Show in 2002.

transportation and could do a lot of the work that a horse would do on a farm, and a dog is much cheaper and easier to care for. The dog could transport a farmer to the barn, help him haul bags of grain, herd cows, ward off predators, keep the farmer company and then cart him home again. No wonder the breed flourished for a time!

However, despite the breed's many abilities, historians presume that the advent of technology put the once-popular Swissy out of work. The breed's numbers dwindled, though they were still certainly in use on farms throughout Europe. Laws were enacted to ensure that the draft dogs were treated ethically, and competitions were created to see what the dogs were truly capable

SENNENHUND BREEDS
The Swissy is a member of the Sennenhund breeds, which also include the Appenzeller and the Entelbucher (both cattle dogs) and the Bernese Mountain Dog. The GSMD is the largest and the oldest of the four breeds, though it was only first entered into regular AKC classes in 1995.

of doing. This enabled the owners of the dogs and the lawmakers to note the limitations of the dogs, figure out how they could make equipment safer and gauge exactly how much the Swissy and other draft breeds were able to pull without endangering their health. It also helped the breed develop as a more successful draft dog, as dogs were bred to do well in these competitions.

Traditionally bred as a draft dog, the Swissy is also a capable sheep herder as demonstrated by Barton Manor's Black Jack.

FINALLY RECOGNIZED

In 1910 the Greater Swiss Mountain Dog was finally recognized by the Swiss Kennel Club. The Swissy, until then considered a short-haired type of the Bernese Mountain Dog, had not been given much attention. At a dog show in 1908, Albert Heim was judging a group of Bernese Mountain Dogs and came across one of these short-haired varieties. He noted how the dog differed from the others and thought that this type should be considered its own breed. With Heim's encouragement, the Greater Swiss Mountain Dog was given its own title, and a breed standard was established. Immediately, efforts began to increase the Swissy's numbers. With the efforts of the new breeders, the first GSMD club was created and the breed slowly began to multiply. It was a slow process, though, with only 50 or so dogs being added to the club's stud book per year throughout the 1930s. It was then, and is still, considered a rare breed in its homeland as well as here in the United States.

Throughout the middle of the 20th century, the breed continued to work as a draft dog. The Swiss Army used the Swissy for draft

Ch. Barton Manor's Brooke, happy to do what Swissys do best—draft work on the farm.

purposes during World War II. With their help and the efforts of others, the Swissy grew in popularity as more people became aware of its existence as a distinct breed and the positive qualities that set it apart from other breeds of dog. At this point, for the first time on record, the number of new Swissy puppies registered every year was over 100. Overall, the number of Swissys in the world had increased to almost 400 by 1945, a vast improvement from 1910 when the Swissy was first recognized as a breed.

THE GREATER SWISS MOUNTAIN DOG COMES TO AMERICA

In 1968, the first Greater Swiss Mountain Dog was brought to the United States by Patricia and Frederick Hoffman and Perrin Rademacher. Together, these three enthusiasts formed the first GSMD club in the United States immediately upon their arrival, the Greater Swiss Mountain Dog Club of America, Inc. (GSMDCA). Howard and Gretel Summons were also an integral part of the creation of this first club in the US. It was their hard work that created the athletic, charismatic stock from which the American Swissy derives today.

The GSMDCA spent years working toward achieving breed recognition by the American Kennel Club (AKC). The club held

its first national specialty in 1983; at that time, the club had a registry of 257 dogs. By 1985 the Greater Swiss Mountain Dog was included in the AKC's Miscellaneous Group. On March 17, 1993 the club transferred their stud records to the AKC, which was used as the foundation for the breed. This record contained over 1,300 dogs. Finally, on July 1, 1995, after 27 years of dedicated work on the part of the GSMDCA, the AKC officially recognized the Greater Swiss Mountain Dog as a breed; the Swissy is included in the AKC's Working Group. Since then, the Swissy has grown in numbers and popularity across the United States. It still remains an obscure breed, but it is more popular than ever before in its history.

Here's a nice example of an American-bred Swissy. This is Ch. Palisades Regal Victoria.

The Swissy has taken nicely to his more recent role as a companion dog.

Today there are around 40 officially recognized Swissy breeders nationwide. Swissy clubs in the United States and Switzerland continue to work together for the betterment of the breed, sending dogs with certain skills or especially good traits back and forth to try and create the highest quality dogs possible. The standard for the breed remains the same in both countries. The physical condition of the dog is still the most important factor for breeders and when dogs are judged at shows. More than anything, the Swissy is a drafting dog, and a solid, muscular body is more important to the integrity of the breed than any other physical trait. There are certain important points, like coat and eye color, but, other than that, the dog's ability to work is what counts in shows and on the farm.

The Swissy is still considered a draft dog, but now the breed competes and participates in a multitude of other events: conformation, agility, search and rescue, obedience, tracking, pack hiking, herding, weight pulling, therapy work and versatility. There are clubs for people interested in training their Swissys for each of these tasks. Clubs provide a great deal of resources for newcomers to these activities.

Considering how recently the Swissy has become a breed and how limited the breed's numbers are in the United States, breed-specific competitions are still being fine-tuned. As of now, there is no draft competition strictly for the GSMD. Instead, they compete with other breeds like the Newfoundland and the Bernese Mountain Dog. There are various distinct titles that the Swissy can earn in competitions, including Draft Dog (DD) and Novice Draft Dog (NDD). The first Swissy to earn one of these titles was Ch. Derby's Eisenhower CD, who earned the NDD from the Bernese Mountain Dog Club of America. Since then, other dogs like Dav-Ka's Cardinal Virtue CD and Ch. Lonestar's Ace CD have gone on to earn their DD titles. The Swissy is certainly stiff competition in drafting contests, with his strong, muscular body and willful determination, but a Swissy's success at drafting is not solely up to the dog. There has to be solid communication between the dog and his owner or handler.

The GSMDCA has started moving toward having an all-Swissy competition, the first step being the creation of the club's own rules and regulations for competition and the training of judges. Rules for a draft competition were written in 1995 and approved in 1998. Since then, several members of the club have taken the steps necessary to be able to judge such a competition, although one has not yet taken place as of this writing.

Another type of competition suited for the Swissy is weight-pulling. The GSMDCA does have its own rules and competitions for this event, but there are also competitions available through the International Weight Pull Association and the United

Kennel Club. As with any competition, the safety of the dogs in weight pulling is the first priority. Dogs must be at least 14 months old to compete and be in good physical condition. Equipment must be appropriate and fit the dog well. Dogs in these competitions can pull over 20 times their body weight across a span of 4 to 6 feet, which is an enormous task.

Since the Swissy is known for being a versatile animal, it seems almost natural that he would be an active competitor in versatility competitions. In these kinds of trials, the Swissy is expected to work with his owner or handler through a variety of tasks including conformation, obedience, drafting, weight pulling, packing, stock work and other activities. This is a sort of decathlon and requires an all-

Ch. Polyanna's Keno proudly shows off the powerful hindquarters required for traditional draft work and more recently, weight pulling.

around athlete with amazing competence in every area.

Dogs working in versatility events should be old enough that strenuous exercise will not harm their developing joints and bones. Throughout the competition dogs are continually monitored to make sure that they are not hurt. These competitions are a chance for the dog to indulge his competitive nature and bond with his favorite people. It's also a chance for the dog to show off his abilities, but competition should, overall, remain fun.

With the proper care and guidance, there is very little this rare newcomer can't accomplish.

There are two types of titles that a Swissy can earn in versatility competition: Versatility Greater Swiss (VGS) and Versatility Greater Swiss Excellent (VSGX). The VGS denotes that a dog has shown a proficiency in several areas. The VSGX denotes that a dog has performed to standards of excellence in several areas. To earn these awards, the dogs must have won a title in conformation, a Companion Dog (CD) title in obedience and two titles from other categories. Winning one of these titles requires a commitment from the dog but also an unwavering desire on the part of the owner, trainer or handler. Dogs alone cannot win these titles.

There is a competition and title built to suit any owner and his dog, but the GSMD as a pet certainly does not have to compete for anything to be a "good" dog. Overall, the Swissy is a big-hearted dog that likes to work hard. The GSMD enjoys working for the people he loves, whether by protecting them, pulling them around in a cart or just by making them laugh. The Swissy seems to fit into any home that offers a lot of careful attention and an understanding of the physical needs specific to the breed. This is a breed sure to grow in popularity in years to come, as it has too much to offer to be ignored.

CHARACTERISTICS OF THE

GREATER SWISS MOUNTAIN DOG

The Greater Swiss Mountain Dog, known in its homeland as *Grosser Schweizer Sennenhund*, is powerful enough to pull a cart of horse feed across the farm by day yet temperate with his family in the evening, playing fetch with the children and cuddling up with everyone in front of the TV. He takes to home life as readily as he takes to cart work, guarding and herding livestock. The Swissy is incredibly versatile, but one thing remains true of these dogs in all situations: they remain constant companions that want nothing more than to spend time with the people they love. This dog will also protect his property with a fierce stance, barking at what he perceives as intruders—guests beware!

The Swissy is a large, tri-colored, double-coated breed known primarily as a draft dog, but also as a herding dog and guard dog. Males are generally between 105 and 140 pounds and 25 to 28 inches tall at the shoulder. Females are slightly smaller, weighing 80 to 110 pounds and being 23 to 27 inches tall at the shoulder. Swissys should be slightly longer than they are tall, with a length to height ratio of 10 to 9; they are certainly not delicate-looking dogs. They are very muscular and heavy-boned, enabling them to do the strenuous work they are known for.

The undercoat of the GSMD is a thick, insulating layer that is

The Greater Swiss Mountain Dog tends to shed his coat, but it is otherwise easy to care for, with regular brushing keeping it in fine shape.

ideally dark gray but may also be light gray or tawny. The black top coat ranges in length from $1^1/_4$ inches to 2 inches long, and the markings are red and white. Though the coat is easy to care for, these dogs shed a lot, especially when they "blow" their coats twice a year. Weekly brushing is recommended.

Most of the dog is black, with white running in a blaze down the forehead and across the muzzle. Red accents the eyebrows of the dog, the undersides of his ears and his cheeks. The neck and chest are also typically white, although patches of white elsewhere are acceptable. Red appears on each leg and white on each foot. The bottom of the dog's tail is red and the tip is white. Symmetry is ideal but not absolutely necessary in the dog's coloring. The only way that a dog's coloring could lead to disqualification in a conformation show is if the dog is not black, red and white. Some dogs are born with a blue or charcoal topcoat or are just red and white. For working dogs and family pets, the texture and length of the Swissy's coat is ideal because it stays clean and attractive with very little maintenance on the owner's part.

The eyes are almond-shaped and brown. Darker brown is preferred, but any brown will do. If either one or both eyes are blue, the dog will be disqualified from conformation showing.

A SWISSY TO WATCH ME
The GSMD is known primarily as a drafting dog, but he is an excellent watchdog as well, alerting the family to any intruders, whether a human or just the neighborhood cat. They generally aren't persistent barkers but will bark up a storm when they perceive trouble.

The tail is not docked but is long and sturdy like the rest of the dog, only tapering at the very tip. The tail does not hinder the working capabilities of the breed. The ears, also undocked, are medium-sized and triangular in shape. Normally the droopy ears stay close to the head, but when the dog's attention is drawn to something, the ears will perk up and the flaps of the ears will move a little forward and slightly away from the head.

The GSMD is a breed made for pulling heavy loads, and its strong hind legs are evidence of that. Consequently, the Swissy is more suited to slow, continuous movement and is built for strength and endurance. The Swissy is better suited for long walks than for runs or sprints. When a Swissy moves, his front legs reach out far in front of him and his strong back legs propel him forward, along with the cart he is pulling. Throughout these movements, the back of the dog remains straight and level.

One distinguishing characteristic of the GSMD is that, unlike other large breeds, the Swissy is dry-mouthed and doesn't drool excessively. This is a very welcome characteristic for people looking to take their dogs on car rides and have drool-free homes. This also makes the Swissy lower maintenance and better smelling than many other dogs of similar stature.

Another quality that sets him apart from other breeds is that the Swissy does not tend to bark unless there's a reason. When he does bark, he has a distinctively loud and deep voice. Normally, the Swissy is fairly quiet unless there's something to bark at, like guests, prowlers or intruding animals.

TEMPERAMENT AND PERSONALITY

The Swissy is described by many as loyal, devoted, strong, industrious, loving, gentle, versatile and eager to please. Of course, every Swissy has his own unique personality and temperament, but the breed, in general, is naturally hard-working, both because Swissys seem to enjoy the exercise and also because they are always looking to help or protect their families. Although the Swissy is a working dog, he very easily adapts to a calm, quiet home life, but he does need considerable exercise. The Swissy is not a "couch potato," especially when young. The GSMD is good with

What big eyes the Greater Swiss has. The Swissy's brown, almond-shaped eyes are all the better to keep a watchful eye on his loving owner.

The gentle Greater Swiss loves little more than spending quality time with the people he loves.

children and other animals, but the manners a dog needs inside the house and socialization skills are something more completely and quickly learned when the owners make a point of exercising and training the dog.

While working, the Swissy remains just as friendly and good-natured as when playing fetch in the backyard. Though no one can know what a Swissy is thinking, the dog certainly seems to enjoy his work, perhaps even thinking of it as a kind of game. These dogs are always eager to help their owners and do not often get stubborn when they are working.

Swissys are quick learners. The ability to pull a cart does not come from instinct alone. However, Swissys develop in the same way that they move, slowly and steadily. It takes around three years for a Swissy to fully mature, making certain things, like house-training, a lengthier process than it is for some other breeds.

The GSMD is also a fantastic family companion. Swissys are incredibly gentle and patient with children. In fact, they tend to like playing with children and feel protective of the children in their families. Even though Swissys are large dogs, they generally seem to recognize that children are small and they act accordingly. They tend not to jump up on kids and generally do not play roughly with them. Although, as a gentle giant, sometimes the Swissy can make the occasional clumsy mistake like hitting a child with his wagging tail, which can be quite a blow for smaller children. For this reason, small children should always be supervised when playing with a Swissy.

Certainly there are things an owner can do to ensure a good dog/child relationship. First, children should be taught to respect the dog, the appropriate way to pick up or handle a puppy and to not hurt or taunt the dog. Also, the earlier you introduce your Swissy to children, the more welcoming and accepting your Swissy will be, although Swissys are generally very accepting of people as a rule.

The GSMD is as accepting of other animals, of all sizes and species, as he is of people. Since the Swissy was developed as a working dog for farmers, he is well behaved and rarely aggressive toward livestock or other dogs—although, as with children, the sooner Swissys are introduced to other animals and the more time they spend around them, the more accepting they will become.

Swissys can become territorial when they are in an enclosed space, barking and jumping to protect that space from strangers. For example, a Swissy locked in a car can do some damage if there are a lot of people walking by. It is not recommended to leave any dog alone in a car, and this is but one more reason why it is unsafe to do so with a Swissy. However, when Swissys are in an open space, they tend to be very amiable.

While the majority of Swissys are incredibly friendly, on occasion it is possible to find one that is a little shy or aggressive. This can be avoided by getting a dog from a reputable breeder and meeting the sire and dam of the puppy to ensure that both have pleasant personalities. Also, with the right socialization early enough in life, these less outgoing dogs can learn better social skills.

Although the Swissy is a working dog, he is a family dog first. Swissys get lonely when they are not with their families and therefore prefer to live in the house with their people instead of in a kennel. Swissys do need space and time to run to get rid of their excess energy, but they are also happy with quiet evenings at home.

TRAINABILITY

The Swissy is a very amiable dog that is eager to please, so positive-reinforcement training works best. Harsher methods have little effect other than to diminish the dog's

The breed's typical coloring can be seen early on in life.

Swissys tend to take longer to mature than some other dogs, so be patient with training—don't skimp on praise and treats.

confidence and take the fun out of training. Swissys love to learn and are happy to perform what their owners ask of them for treats and praise.

Swissys take rather well to clicker training, which allows a dog to more immediately connect the action with the reward. Swissys are smart and learn quickly, but it's best to avoid distractions and keep lessons short so that the dog is always focused on the task at hand. Also, consistency is crucial. Being inconsistent with your training methods will only confuse the dog and make the training process much longer.

House-training the Swissy might take longer than some owners would like. As a large,

strong dog, the Swissy develops slowly over a longer period of time. But, at about three months of age, the puppy is ready to begin house-training. Noticing the signs of "having to go" requires a good amount of attention and sensitivity on the part of the owner. A Swissy puppy may be seven to nine months old before he is basically house-trained but, since the puppy is still maturing, the owner will have to be patient when the occasional accident happens.

It seems that no one can quite agree exactly how old the GSMD should be to begin training to pull a cart. Some say as young as 6 months; some say 18 months, but an owner should really talk to his dog's veterinarian to see if the dog is ready. If training begins too soon, it could be damaging to the development of the dog's joints and cause problems later in life.

When the Swissy is ready to learn to pull a cart, begin the training process by building the dog's muscles. This can be done through long walks—the Swissy is not built for running. Then the dog should learn the feel of the cart. Once the dog begins to feel comfortable pulling the cart, weight can be added slowly, allowing the dog to work up to heavy loads. A dog with experience pulling a cart can pull ten times or more his own body weight.

Training a Swissy to pull a cart requires a lot of commitment on the part of the owner. Proper equipment must always be used for the safety of the dog, and equipment can be expensive. Also, training must be consistent, which requires an owner to dedicate significant amounts of time to this endeavor.

Because the GSMD has draft work in his blood, it can sometimes be difficult to train him to walk nicely on a leash. This dog tends to pull, and a smaller owner may be dragged down the block unless a lot of training is done with the leash. Swissys also tend to want to be "dominant" in the pack order, so it's important to socialize a pup early so that he understands that his job isn't to run the show.

HEALTH CONCERNS

The GSMD is susceptible to a variety of health problems related to size and genetics: hip dysplasia, elbow dysplasia, osteochondritis dissecans (which affects the shoulders), gastric torsion (bloat), splenic torsion, epilepsy, distichiasis and entropion (the latter two affecting the eyes). The top causes of death among Swissys include epilepsy, bloat, splenic torsion and various types of cancers. Since the Swissy is susceptible to various diseases, some hereditary and others not, the owner must be knowledgeable about these disorders before bringing a Swissy into his life and must do his best to ensure that his puppy comes from healthy stock. Caring for a sick dog requires a lot of time, love and patience, and the owner should have the means to get medical care for the dog if necessary and must make the commitment to care for his dog if unforeseen medical problems develop.

Do whatever is in your power to keep your Swissy healthy. Your Swissy looks to you for all of his needs.

DO YOU KNOW ABOUT HIP DYSPLASIA?

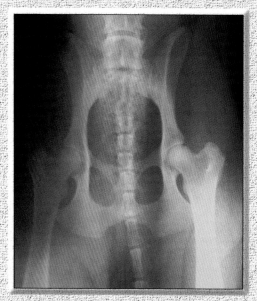

X-ray of a dog with "Good" hips.

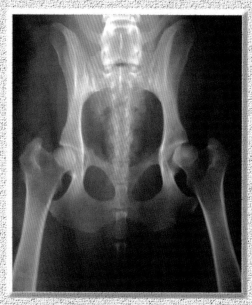

X-ray of a dog with "Moderate" dysplastic hips.

Hip dysplasia is a fairly common condition found in pure-bred dogs. When a dog has hip dysplasia, his hind leg has an incorrectly formed hip joint. By constant use of the hip joint, it becomes more and more loose, wears abnormally and may become arthritic.

Hip dysplasia can only be confirmed with an x-ray, but certain symptoms may indicate a problem. Your dog may have a hip dysplasia problem if he walks in a peculiar manner, hops instead of smoothly runs, uses his hind legs in unison (to keep the pressure off the weak joint), has trouble getting up from a prone position or always sits with both legs together on one side of his body.

As the dog matures, he may adapt well to life with a bad hip, but in a few years the arthritis develops and many dogs with hip dysplasia become crippled.

Hip dysplasia is considered an inherited disease and can be diagnosed definitively by x-ray only when the dog is two years old, although symptoms often appear earlier. Some experts claim that a special diet might help your puppy outgrow the bad hip, but the usual treatments are surgical. The removal of the pectineus muscle, the removal of the round part of the femur, reconstructing the pelvis and replacing the hip with an artificial one are all surgical interventions that are expensive, but they are usually very successful. Follow the advice of your veterinarian.

Swissys are prone to genetic dysplasia, which happens when cartilage in the joint forms abnormally, causing arthritis. This is most commonly found in the hips but also can be seen in the elbow joints. When choosing a puppy, use a reputable breeder that takes precautions to avoid this condition by selective breeding. The sire and dam of your puppy should be certified by the Orthopedic Foundation for Animals (OFA) as having hips and elbows in "good" or "excellent" condition. This rating should be listed on their papers and is also available by contacting the OFA. In 2004, the OFA tested 1,246 Swissys for hip dysplasia; of those dogs, 10.7 percent proved to be in "excellent" condition and 19.4 percent were dysplastic. Overall, 77.8 percent of the dogs' hips were in normal working order.

Osteochondritis dissecans (OCD) is a similar problem affecting the dog's shoulders. This is at least partly genetic, so choosing a puppy from healthy parents with OFA clearances for OCD and related problems is important for this reason as well. However, this disorder can possibly be prevented by proper nutrition and exercise, so it is essential to take good care of this breed. To prevent joint problems, Swissy puppies should not be encouraged to jump from high places or run a lot, as both can be jarring to developing joints.

It is crucial that all Swissy owners learn the symptoms of bloat, a disorder that primarily affects larger and deep-chested breeds and is a major cause of death in the GSMD. Also known as gastric torsion, this condition occurs when a dog's stomach fills with air and twists, cutting off oxygen to other organs. The dog may appear uncomfortable and try to vomit. As the stomach swells, the torso of the dog might become enlarged and will feel hardened. There is no single cause of bloat, so there is no concrete way to prevent it other than to be very careful about feeding and exercise practices. Veterinarians recommend feeding two smaller meals a day rather than one large meal. Also, limit exercise for about two hours before and after meals. If bloat should occur, the only way to correct the problem is surgery; if

THE DANGERS OF BLOAT

One of the biggest health problems for the Swissy is bloat. Careful feeding and exercise practices should help avoid this often deadly condition, in which the stomach twists unnaturally and cuts off blood flow to the other organs. It is important that Swissy owners educate themselves about the condition and its symptoms, preventives and treatment. Discuss bloat with your breeder and with your vet and do all you can to protect your Swissy.

the dog is not operated on quickly enough, and that means *immediately*, bloat is fatal. More on preventives and recognizing symptoms is discussed in the chapter on proper care.

Splenic torsion is a condition in which the spleen twists, completely blocking the vein that drains the blood but still allowing blood to be pumped into the organ. This causes the spleen to become engorged with blood and enlarged, sometimes as much as several times its normal size. As this happens, blood clots develop and the spleen eventually dies. This is a very painful condition and often causes an affected dog to go into shock. Symptoms include pale gums, overall weakness, inappetence and a distended abdomen. Sometimes you can detect a hardened mass by feeling the abdomen. Dogs displaying these symptoms must see a vet immediately. An affected dog's condition must be stabilized, his heart condition monitored and surgery, called a splenectomy, performed to remove the spleen. As with gastric torsion, this condition is fatal if veterinary attention is not sought in time and is one of the major health concerns and causes of death in the GSMD.

Epilepsy is another disorder to which the GSMD is genetically predisposed and another reason why breeders must carefully choose the sire and dam for every Swissy litter. Other illnesses can make epilepsy more likely, so keeping the Swissy healthy is very important. Different types of epilepsy and seizures can be seen and causes are not always known. Sometimes the onset of seizures in

It is now thought that elevated bowls could increase the risk of bloat. Since your Swissy is a deep-chested breed, you must take bloat preventives into consideration; consult your vet.

the Swissy does not occur until later in life, presenting an issue for breeders, as sometimes epilepsy will present in a dog or bitch after he or she has already been bred. Another challenge is that while epilepsy can be managed with medication, some Swissys do not respond to this treatment or suffer serious side effects. The treatment or the seizures themselves can be fatal. Reducing the occurrence of epilepsy in the breed is a major focus in GSMD health research and a major concern of Swissy breeders.

THE IDEAL OWNER

The ideal owner for the GSMD is a family or individual who lives either in the suburbs or on a farm; either situation requires a fenced yard. This breed loves to chase other animals, so a squirrel or neighborhood cat can cause the dog to take off, and you want your Swissy to stay safely at home. Also, because these dogs were originally bred to work in mountainous regions, they do best in cooler climes. They suffer when they get too hot and can get heat stroke. They do fine in warmer regions as long as they have a cool place to spend time during the heat of the day.

Owners of a Swissy must be eager to spend time with their dog; owners cannot keep a Swissy outdoors in a kennel. The Swissy is a good addition to a family with

The ideal Greater Swiss owner will be someone ready and willing to spend plenty of quality time outside with her pet.

children or other pets, but take caution when introducing an older dog to smaller pets. Farmers will enjoy how the Swissy helps with draft work and provides excellent protection against intruders.

It's important that owners of a Swissy, especially a Swissy puppy, realize the limitations of their dog. A Swissy is neither a good running companion nor a good dog for someone who travels a lot. He will not be a good pet for someone with a small apartment. The Swissy does need exercise, so long walks are great. This breed also requires a very consistent and nutritious diet.

Swissy owners need not teach the dog to be a draft dog or have him work in any other way, but he

The Swissy will prove to be an excellent companion dog, as evidenced by his gentle expression, but is also an extremely versatile dog that will thrive in work and play.

can be useful. It would be nice for the Swissy to find a home with someone also interested in these same things. However, this breed can be happy as a house dog as long as he has owners who will keep him active and share their lives with him. However, this breed isn't great for first-time dog owners. A more experienced owner is best, as these dogs can be challenging.

A breeder is the best way to secure a new Swissy for several reasons. A good breeder is dedicated to producing a healthy line of dogs, a line that is continuously more physically fit to pull carts and that has a solid temperament. When you go to a good breeder, you can be relatively sure that you'll get a good puppy. Furthermore, if you think you might be interested in showing your dog or training him for competition, it is important to get a registered Swissy from a responsible breeder. Another reason for going to a quality breeder to get a dog is that the GSMD is a relatively rare breed in the United States and even in its native country of Switzerland. There are only a limited number of puppies born every year. If you don't go to a quality breeder, it may be difficult to find a well-bred, healthy Swissy elsewhere. That being said, though, there are other reputable ways to obtain a Swissy, such as through rescue organizations, which are usually run by breed clubs and breeders.

You probably won't find a Swissy breeder right around the corner. They are scattered across the United States. The Greater Swiss Mountain Dog Club of America (www.gsmdca.org) can help interested people locate the breeder nearest them. Before beginning a breeder and puppy search, however, a prospective owner must realize that no matter his intentions for his dog, be it pet, working or competition, a Swissy is a huge emotional investment. Once Swissys are trained and fully into adulthood, they are rather self-reliant, but the road through puppyhood can be a lengthy one for the Swissy, and owners need to have patience. And no matter the age of the Swissy, he always needs lots of love and attention from his family.

RESCUE
Swissys that find themselves in need of new homes for whatever reason often end up in the care of rescue organizations, as dogs of all breeds do. Once again, the Swissy is a relatively rare breed, so the number of Swissys available through rescue organizations is certainly limited. A rescue group may be a good option for families who are looking for a Swissy just as a good pet. Rescued Swissys might have more emotional problems than your average GSMD, so a rescued dog will require a little more sensitivity on the owner's part, and perhaps a little more training too, but it is certainly possible to find a great family pet through a rescue organization. There are a number of reasons why a Swissy might end up at a rescue organization, many of which have little to do with the dog and more to do with the lifestyle of his previous owners.

There are a variety of rescue organizations for the GSMD. The Greater Swiss Mountain Dog Club of America and regional Swissy organizations can put you in touch with these groups.

GREATER SWISS MOUNTAIN DOG

WHAT IS A BREED STANDARD?
A breed standard is an official document drawn up by a breed's parent club (in this case the GSMDCA) and approved by the registering kennel club (in this case the AKC). This document provides a written description of the ideal characteristics of the breed: the physical traits, personality, movement and inherent abilities that make the breed what it is and distinguish it from other breeds. Guidelines like this are indispensable to breeders as they strive to preserve their breed in its true form from generation to generation, as well as to conformation show judges as they choose the dog that best represents the ideal of the breed as the winner.

Of course, words are open to individual interpretation, so one must learn to recognize what the words in the standard mean by observing quality Greater Swiss Mountain Dogs in action. Following is the AKC standard for the GSMD.

THE AMERICAN KENNEL CLUB BREED STANDARD FOR THE GREATER SWISS MOUNTAIN DOG

General Appearance: The Greater Swiss Mountain Dog is a Draft and Drover breed and should structurally appear as such. It is a striking, tri-colored, large, powerful, confident dog of sturdy appearance. It is a heavy boned and well muscled dog which, in spite of its size and weight, is agile enough to perform the all-purpose farm duties of the mountainous regions of its origin.

Illustration showing dog of correct type, balance, structure, substance and typical tri-color marking pattern.

Size, Proportion and Substance: Height at the highest point of the shoulder is ideally: Dogs 25.5 to 28.5 inches. Bitches 23.5 to 27 inches. Body length to height is approximately a 10 to 9 proportion, thus appearing slightly longer than tall. It is a heavy boned and well muscled dog of sturdy appearance.

Head: *Expression* is animated and gentle. The *eyes* are almond shaped and brown, dark brown preferred, medium sized, neither deep set nor protruding. Blue eye or eyes is a disqualification. Eyelids are close fitting and eyerims are black. The *ears* are medium sized, set high, triangular in shape, gently rounded at the tip and hang close to the head when in repose. When alert, the ears are brought forward and raised at the base. The top of the ear is

Illustration of head study showing correct type, structure and proportion.

level with the top of the skull. The *skull* is flat and broad with a slight stop. The backskull and muzzle are of approximately equal length. The backskull is approximately twice the width of the muzzle. The *muzzle* is large, blunt and straight, not pointed and most often with a slight rise before the end. In adult dogs the nose leather is always black. The lips are clean and as a dry-mouthed breed, flews are only slightly developed. The *teeth* meet in a scissors bite.

Typical Swissy coloration is black and white with rust points seen over each eye, on the cheeks and elsewhere as indicated by the standard.

Neck, Topline and Body: The neck is of moderate length, strong, muscular and clean. The topline is level from the withers to the croup. The chest is deep and broad with a slight

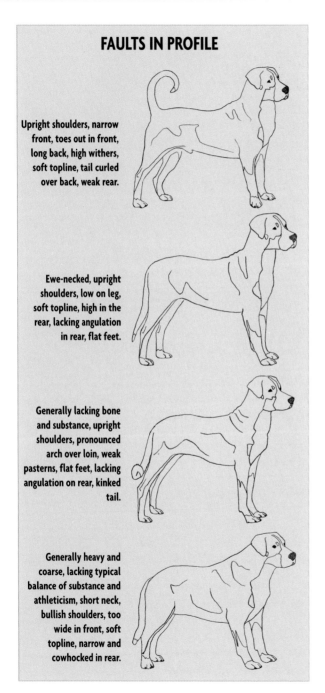

FAULTS IN PROFILE

Upright shoulders, narrow front, toes out in front, long back, high withers, soft topline, tail curled over back, weak rear.

Ewe-necked, upright shoulders, low on leg, soft topline, high in the rear, lacking angulation in rear, flat feet.

Generally lacking bone and substance, upright shoulders, pronounced arch over loin, weak pasterns, flat feet, lacking angulation on rear, kinked tail.

Generally heavy and coarse, lacking typical balance of substance and athleticism, short neck, bullish shoulders, too wide in front, soft topline, narrow and cowhocked in rear.

protruding breastbone. The ribs are well-sprung. Depth of chest is approximately one half the total height of the dog at the withers. Body is full with slight tuck up. The loins are broad and strong. The croup is long, broad and smoothly rounded to the tail insertion. The tail is thick from root to tip, tapering slightly at the tip, reaching to the hocks and carried down in repose. When alert and in movement, the tail may be carried higher and slightly curved upwards, but should not curl, or tilt over the back. The bones of the tail should feel straight.

Forequarters: The shoulders are long, sloping, strong and moderately laid back. They are flat and well-muscled. Forelegs are straight and strong. The pasterns slope very slightly, but are not weak. Feet are round and compact with well arched toes, and turn neither in nor out. The dewclaws may or may not be present.

Hindquarters: The thighs are broad, strong and muscular. The stifles are moderately bent and taper smoothly into the hocks. The hocks are well let down and straight when viewed from the rear. Feet are round and compact with well arched toes, and turn neither in nor out. Dewclaws should be removed.

Coat: Topcoat is dense, approximately 1 1/4 to 2 inches in length. Undercoat must be present and may be thick and sometimes showing, almost always present at neck but may be present throughout. Color of undercoat ranges from the preferred dark gray to light gray to tawny. Total absence of undercoat is undesirable and should be penalized.

Color: The topcoat is black. The markings are rich rust and white. Symmetry of markings is desired. On the head, rust typically appears over each eye, on each cheek and on the underside of the ears. On the body, rust appears on both sides of the forechest, on all four legs and underneath the tail. White markings appear typically on the head (blaze) and muzzle. The blaze may vary in length and width. It may be a very thin stripe or wider band. The blaze may extend just barely to the stop or may extend over the top of the skull and may meet with a white patch or collar on the neck. Typically, white appears on the chest, running unbroken from the throat to the chest, as well as on all four feet and on the tip of the tail. White patches or collar on the neck is acceptable. Any color other than the "Black, Red and White" tricolored dog described above, such as "Blue/Charcoal, Red and White" or "Red and White" is considered a disqualification. When evaluating the Greater Swiss Mountain Dog, markings and other cosmetic factors should be considered of lesser importance than other aspects of type which directly affect working ability.

Gait: Good reach in front, powerful drive in rear. Movement with a level back.

Temperament: Bold, faithful, willing worker. Alert and vigilant. Shyness or aggressiveness shall be severely penalized.

Summary: The foregoing is the description of the ideal Greater Swiss Mountain Dog. Defects of both structure and temperament are to be judged more severely than mere lack of elegance because they reduce the animal's capacity to work. Any fault that detracts from the above described working dog should be penalized to the extent of the deviation.

Disqualifications: Any color other than the "Black, Red and White" tri-colored dog described above, such as "Blue/Charcoal, Red and White" or "Red and White." Blue eye or eyes.

Approved: April 8, 2003
Effective: May 29, 2003

GREATER SWISS MOUNTAIN DOG

CHOOSING A PUPPY

When choosing a Swissy puppy, first consider what you're looking for in a dog. Which sex would you prefer? Are you looking to show your dog, work with your dog or compete in performance events with your dog, or do you just want a pet? Is it important that your dog lives up to the ideal described in his breed standard?

Observe the breeder's interaction with her dogs. The dogs' affection toward the breeder tells volumes about how she cares for them.

No matter your answers to these questions, everyone wants a healthy dog. To give you the best chance at acquiring a Swissy that will remain healthy throughout his life, find a reputable breeder and ask lots of questions. Contact the GSMDCA and ask them to refer you to member breeders in your region, as these breeders must adhere to the club's code of ethics in their breeding programs, which include rules about health screening, puppy upbringing, sales conduct and more. A prospective owner who is looking for a new puppy should learn about the history of the puppy's parents. Specifically, ask the breeder about hip and elbow dysplasia, epilepsy, OCD

PRECOCIOUS PUPPIES

Swissy pups are a handful and can be "mouthy," testing everything in the world with those sharp teeth. A new owner should be prepared to begin socialization and training right away. Puppy kindergarten and individual training are great ideas.

Have fun meeting the pups and be sure to meet at least one of the parents too. The best indicator of your puppy's soundness, in health and personality, is the parents of the puppy you intend to acquire.

(osteochondritis dissecans) and eye problems. Ask if dogs of his bloodline have had problems with gastric or splenic torsion. The hereditary components of the latter two disorders are not known, but some feel that affected dogs should not be bred.

Meet the dam of the litter and the sire, if he is on the premises, to see if you like their personalities. If the dam is not available for you to meet, continue your search elsewhere. It is common for the sire to not be with the litter, but the pups should be with their mother until they leave for new homes. Watch how the breeder and all of his dogs relate to each other and note how the dogs interact with you as a stranger. If the parents are not friendly and personable, then their puppies may not be either, though socialization in this breed counts for a lot.

Both male and female Swissy puppies have the same loving personality. The main difference

A rare find indeed—a blue Swissy puppy in a litter of black brethren.

between males and females is in their size. If you're looking for a Swissy on the smaller end of the spectrum, then a female is best, but unless size is a factor, sex really is not of much importance in this breed.

A puppy is a big commitment, emotionally and financially, so it is important for people looking to add a puppy to their family to do their homework. A friendly and healthy Swissy puppy will make it worth the work!

MAKE A COMMITMENT

Dogs are most assuredly man's best friend, but they are also a lot of work. When you add a puppy to your family, you also are adding to your daily responsibilities for years to come. Dogs need more than just food, water and a place to sleep. They also require training (which can be ongoing throughout the lifetime of the dog), activity to keep them physically and mentally fit and hands-on attention every day, plus grooming and healthcare. Your life as you now know it may well disappear! Are you prepared for such drastic changes?

A COMMITTED NEW OWNER

By now you should understand what makes the Greater Swiss Mountain Dog a most unique and special dog, one that may fit nicely into your family and lifestyle. If you have researched breeders, you should be able to recognize a knowledgeable and responsible GSMD breeder who cares not only about his pups but also about what kind of owner you will be. If you have completed the final step in your new journey, you have found a litter, or possibly two, of quality Greater Swiss Mountain Dog pups.

A visit with the puppies and their breeder should be an education in itself. Breed research, breeder selection and puppy visitation are very important aspects of finding the puppy of your dreams. Beyond that, these things also lay the foundation for a successful future with your pup. Puppy personalities within each litter vary, from the shy and easygoing puppy to the one who is dominant and assertive, with most pups falling somewhere in between. By spending time with the puppies you will be able to recognize certain behaviors and what these behaviors indicate about each pup's temperament. Which type of pup will complement your family dynamics is best determined by observing the puppies in action within their "pack." Your breeder's expertise and recommendations are also valuable. Although you may fall in love with a bold and brassy male, the breeder may suggest that another pup would be best for you. The breeder's experience in rearing Swissy pups and matching their temperaments with appropriate humans offers the best assurance that your pup will meet your needs and expectations. The type of puppy that you select is just as important as your decision that the Greater Swiss Mountain Dog is the breed for you.

The decision to live with a Swissy is a serious commitment and not one to be taken lightly. This puppy is a living sentient being that will be dependent on you for basic survival for his entire life. Beyond the basics of survival—food, water, shelter and protection—he needs much, much more. The new pup needs love, nurturing and a proper canine education to mold him into a responsible, well-behaved canine citizen. Your Swissy's health and

Only the most experienced dog owner should consider being in charge of a whole pack!

good manners will need consistent monitoring and regular "tune-ups," so your job as a responsible dog owner will be ongoing throughout every stage of his life. If you are not prepared to accept these responsibilities and commit to them for the next decade, then you are not prepared to own a dog of any breed.

Although the responsibilities

A puppy relies on you not only for food and water but also for constant guidance and attention.

Water is essential for adults and pups alike. Pay attention to when your pup eats and drinks so you will know when he needs to relieve himself.

of owning a dog may at times tax your patience, the joy of living with your Swissy far outweighs the workload, and a well-mannered adult dog is worth your time and effort. Before your very eyes, your new charge will grow up to be your most loyal friend, devoted to you unconditionally.

YOUR SWISSY SHOPPING LIST

Just as expectant parents prepare a nursery for their baby, so should you ready your home for the arrival of your Swissy pup. If you have the necessary puppy supplies purchased and in place before he comes home, it will ease the puppy's transition from the warmth and familiarity of his mom and littermates to the brand-new environment of his new home and human family. You will be too busy to stock up and prepare your house after your pup comes home, that's for sure. Imagine how a pup must feel upon being transported to a strange new place. It's up to you to comfort him and to let your little pup know that he is going to be happy with you.

FOOD AND WATER BOWLS

Your puppy will need separate bowls for his food and water. Stainless steel bowls are generally preferred over plastic bowls since they sterilize better and pups are less inclined to chew on the metal. Heavy-duty ceramic bowls are popular, but consider how often you will have to pick up those heavy bowls. Buy adult-sized pans, as your puppy will grow into them quickly.

THE DOG CRATE

If you think that crates are tools of punishment and confinement for when a dog has misbehaved, think again. Most breeders and almost all trainers recommend a crate as the preferred house-

training aid as well as for all-around puppy training and safety. Because dogs are natural den creatures that prefer cave-like environments, the benefits of crate use are many. The crate provides the puppy with his very own "safe house," a cozy place to sleep, take a break or seek comfort with a favorite toy; a travel aid to house your dog when on the road, at motels or at the vet's office; a training aid to help teach your puppy proper toileting habits; and a place of solitude when non-dog people happen to drop by and don't want a lively puppy—or even a well-behaved adult dog—saying hello or begging for attention.

Crates come in several types, although the wire crate and the fiberglass airline-type crate are the most popular. Both are safe and your puppy will adjust to either one, so the choice is up to you. The wire crates offer better visibility for the pup as well as better ventilation. Many of the wire crates easily collapse into suitcase-size carriers. The fiberglass crates, similar to those used by the airlines for animal transport, are sturdier and more den-like. However, the fiberglass crates do not collapse and are less ventilated than a wire crate, which can be problematic in hot weather. Some of the newer crates are made of heavy plastic mesh; they are very lightweight and fold

The Greater Swiss will accept his crate as his home away from home in no time. Crate training pays countless dividends in training and safety.

up into slim-line suitcases. However, a mesh crate might not be suitable for a pup with manic chewing habits.

Don't bother with a puppy-sized crate. Although your Greater Swiss Mountain Dog will be a little fellow when you bring him home, he will grow up in the blink of an eye and your puppy crate will be useless. Purchase a crate that will accommodate an adult GSMD. A Swissy can stand anywhere from 23 to 28.5 inches at the shoulder, depending on sex and individual dog, so an extra-large crate will be necessary. One that measures about 48 inches long by 30 inches wide by 36 inches high should do nicely.

TOYS 'R SAFE

The vast array of tantalizing puppy toys is staggering. Stroll through any pet shop or pet-supply outlet and you will see that the choices can be overwhelming. However, not all dog toys are safe or sensible. Most very young puppies enjoy soft woolly toys that they can snuggle with and carry around. (You know they have outgrown them when they shred them up!) Avoid toys that have buttons, tabs or other enhancements that can be chewed off and swallowed. Soft toys that squeak are fun, but make sure your puppy does not disembowel the toy and remove (and swallow) the squeaker. Toys that rattle or make noise can excite a puppy, but they present the same danger as the squeaky kind and so require supervision. Hard rubber toys that bounce can also entertain a pup, but make sure that the toy is too big for your pup to swallow.

BEDDING AND CRATE PADS

Your puppy will enjoy some type of soft bedding in his "room" (the crate), something he can snuggle into to feel cozy and secure. Old towels or blankets are good choices for a young pup, since he may (and probably will) have a toileting accident or two in the crate or decide to chew on the bedding material. Once he is fully trained and out of the early chewing stage, you can replace the puppy bedding with a permanent crate pad if you prefer. Crate pads and other dog beds run the gamut from inexpensive to high-end doggie-designer styles, but don't splurge on the good stuff until you are sure that your puppy is reliable and won't tear it up or make a mess on it.

PUPPY TOYS

Just as infants and older children require objects to stimulate their minds and bodies, puppies need toys to entertain their curious brains, wiggly paws and achy teeth. A fun array of safe doggie toys will help satisfy your puppy's chewing instincts and distract him from gnawing on the leg of your antique chair or your new leather sofa. Most puppy toys are cute and look as if they would be a lot of fun, but not all are necessarily safe or good for your puppy, so use caution when you go puppy-toy shopping.

Swissy puppies are known to

put their mouths on everything they can find, so provide plenty of safe toys and encourage proper chewing from the outset. The best "chewcifiers" are nylon and hard rubber bones, which are safe to gnaw on and come in sizes appropriate for all age groups and breeds. Be especially careful of natural bones, which can splinter or develop dangerous sharp edges; pups can easily swallow or choke on those bone splinters. Veterinarians often tell of surgical nightmares involving bits of splintered bone, because in addition to the danger of choking, the sharp pieces can damage the intestinal tract.

Similarly, rawhide chews, while a favorite of most dogs and puppies, can be equally dangerous. Pieces of rawhide are easily swallowed after they get soft and gummy from chewing, and dogs have been known to choke on pieces of ingested rawhide. Rawhide chews should be offered only when you can supervise the puppy.

Soft woolly toys are special puppy favorites. They come in a wide variety of cute shapes and sizes; some look like little stuffed animals. Puppies love to shake them up and toss them about or simply carry them around. Be careful of fuzzy toys that have button eyes or noses that your pup could chew off and swallow, and make sure that he does not disembowel a squeaky toy to remove the squeaker. Braided

Introduce your Swissy to safe chew toys as a pup to encourage proper chewing behavior as he grows.

Think twice before buying a puppy-sized crate for your Greater Swiss Mountain Dog. He will outgrow a small crate before you know it.

Purchase a collar
that can expand
with the puppy's
growth, and
check it regularly
for proper fit.

rope toys are similar in that they are fun to chew and toss around, but they shred easily and the strings are easy to swallow. The strings are not digestible and, if the puppy doesn't pass them in his stool, he could end up at the vet's office. As with rawhides, your puppy should be closely monitored with rope toys.

If you believe that your pup has ingested a piece of one of his toys, check his stool for the next couple of days to see if he passes the item when he defecates. At the same time, also watch for signs of intestinal distress. A call to your veterinarian might be in order to get his advice and be on the safe side.

An all-time favorite toy for puppies (young and old!) is the empty gallon milk jug. Hard plastic juice containers—46 ounces or more—are also excellent. Such containers make lots of noise when they are batted about, and puppies go crazy with delight as they play with them. However, they don't often last very long, so be sure to remove and replace them when they start to get chewed up.

A word of caution about homemade toys: be careful with your choices of non-traditional play objects. Never use old shoes or socks, since a puppy cannot distinguish between the old ones on which he's allowed to chew and the new ones in your closet that are strictly off limits. That principle applies to anything that resembles something that you don't want your puppy to chew.

COLLARS

A lightweight nylon collar is the best choice for a very young pup. Quick-click collars are easy to put on and remove, and they can be adjusted as the puppy grows. Introduce him to his collar as soon as he comes home to get him accustomed to wearing it. He'll get used to it quickly and won't mind a bit. Make sure that it is snug enough that it won't slip off yet loose enough to be comfortable for the pup. You should be able to slip two fingers between the collar and his neck. Check the

out for toileting you will want to keep him in the specific area chosen for his potty spot.

Once the puppy is heel-trained with a traditional leash, you can consider purchasing a retractable lead. A retractable lead is good for walking adult dogs that are already leash-wise. This type of lead allows the dog to roam farther away from you and explore a wider area when out walking and also retracts when you need to keep him close to you. You do have to be careful that you purchase a retractable lead that is sturdy enough to withstand your adult Swissy's weight; buy the strongest one you can find.

This Greater Swiss pup is getting an introduction to his leash. Walking on lead will take time and proper training, but a tasty treat will make it a pleasant experience for him.

collar often, as puppies grow in spurts, and his collar can become too tight almost overnight. Choke collars are for training purposes but are not recommended for use on the Swissy. With this breed, positive reinforcement will get results while physical corrections will only erode the dog's confidence in you as his leader.

LEASHES

A 6-foot nylon lead is an excellent choice for a young puppy. It is lightweight and not as tempting to chew as a leather lead. You can switch to a 6-foot leather lead after your pup has grown and is used to walking politely on a lead. For initial puppy walks and house-training purposes, you should invest in a shorter lead so that you have more control over the puppy. At first, you don't want him wandering too far away from you, and when taking him

A new collar, new leash and new toys all for a brand new pup! As with all new things, both you and your pup have some things to get used to, and you will.

HOME SAFETY FOR YOUR PUPPY

The importance of puppy-proofing cannot be overstated. In addition to making your house comfortable for your Swissy's arrival, you also must make sure that your house is safe for your puppy before you bring him home. There are countless hazards in the owner's personal living environment that a pup can sniff, chew, swallow or destroy. Many are obvious; others are not. Do a thorough advance house check to remove or rearrange those things that could hurt your puppy, keeping any potentially dangerous items out of areas to which he will have access.

Electrical cords are especially dangerous, since puppies view them as irresistible chew toys. Unplug and remove all exposed cords or fasten them beneath

KEEP OUT OF REACH

Most dogs don't browse around your medicine cabinet, but accidents do happen! The drug acetaminophen, the active ingredient in certain over-the-counter pain relievers, can be deadly to dogs and cats if ingested in large quantities. Acetaminophen toxicity, caused by the dog's swallowing 15 to 20 tablets, can be manifested in abdominal pains within a day or two of ingestion, as well as liver damage. If you suspect your dog has swiped a bottle of medication, get the dog to the vet immediately so that the vet can induce vomiting and cleanse the dog's stomach.

baseboards where the puppy cannot reach them. Veterinarians and firefighters can tell you horror stories about electrical burns and house fires that resulted from puppy-chewed electrical cords. Consider this a most serious precaution for your puppy and the rest of your family.

Scout your home for tiny objects that might be seen at a pup's eye level. Keep medication bottles and cleaning supplies well out of reach, and do the same with waste baskets and other trash containers. It goes without saying that you should not use rodent poison or other toxic chemicals in any puppy area and that you must keep such containers safely locked up. You will be amazed at

There are plenty of objects in and around your home that can cause your Greater Swiss pup injury. Make sure your house and yard are properly puppy-proofed before he arrives.

how many places a curious puppy can discover!

Once your house has cleared inspection, check your yard. A sturdy fence, well embedded into the ground, will give your dog a safe place to play and potty. Swissys are curious and athletic dogs, so a fence of at least 6 feet high is required to safely contain an agile youngster or adult. Check the fence periodically for necessary repairs. If there is a weak link or space to squeeze through, you can be sure a determined Swissy will discover it.

The garage and shed can be hazardous places for a pup, as things like fertilizers, chemicals and tools are usually kept there. It's best to keep these areas off limits to the pup. Antifreeze is especially dangerous to dogs, as they find the taste appealing and it takes only a few licks from the driveway to kill a dog, puppy or adult, small breed or large.

VISITING THE VETERINARIAN

A good veterinarian is your GSMD puppy's best health-insurance policy. If you do not already have a vet, ask friends and experienced dog people in your area for recommendations so that you can select a vet before you bring your GSMD puppy home. A vet who is familiar with large breeds and with the Swissy's specific health concerns is a good idea. Also

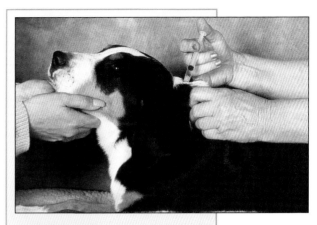

ASK THE VET
Help your vet help you to become a well-informed dog owner. Don't be shy about becoming involved in your puppy's veterinary care by asking questions and gaining as much knowledge as you can. For starters, ask what shots your puppy is getting and what diseases they prevent, and discuss with your vet the safest way to vaccinate. Find out what is involved in your dog's annual wellness visits. If you plan to spay or neuter, discuss the best age at which to have this done. Start out on the right "paw" with your puppy's vet and develop good communication with him, as he will care for your dog's health throughout the dog's entire life.

arrange for your puppy's first veterinary examination beforehand, since many vets have two- and three-week waiting periods and your puppy should visit the vet within a day or so of coming home.

It's important to make sure your puppy's first visit to the vet is a pleasant and positive one. The vet should take great care to befriend the pup and handle him gently to make their first meeting a positive experience. The vet will give the pup a thorough physical examination and set up a schedule for vaccinations and other necessary wellness visits. Be sure to show your vet any health and inoculation records, which you should have received from your breeder. Your vet is a great source of canine health information, so be sure to ask questions and take notes. Creating a health journal for your puppy will make a handy reference for his wellness and any future health problems that may arise.

MEETING THE FAMILY

Your Greater Swiss Mountain Dog's homecoming is an exciting time for all members of the family,

---

MEET AND MINGLE
Puppies need to meet people and see the world if they are to grow up confident and unafraid. Take your puppy with you on everyday outings and errands. On-lead walks around the neighborhood and to the park offer the pup good exposure to the goings-on of his new human world. Avoid areas frequented by other dogs until your puppy has had his full round of puppy shots; ask your vet when your pup will be properly protected. Arrange for your puppy to meet new people of all ages every week.

---

and it's only natural that everyone will be eager to meet him, pet him and play with him. However, for the puppy's sake, it's best to make these initial family meetings as uneventful as possible so that the pup is not overwhelmed with too much too soon. Remember, he has just left his dam and his litter-mates and is away from the breeder's home for the first time. Despite his fuzzy wagging tail, he is still apprehensive and wondering where he is and who all these strange humans are. It's best to let him explore on his own and meet the family members as he feels comfortable. Let him investigate all the new smells, sights and sounds at his own pace. Children should be especially careful to not get overly excited, use loud voices or hug

Bringing a Swissy into your home is the beginning of a beautiful friendship.

the pup too tightly. Be calm, gentle and affectionate, and be ready to comfort him if he appears frightened or uneasy.

Be sure to show your puppy his new crate during this first day home. Toss a treat or two inside the crate; if he associates the crate with food, he will associate the crate with good things. If he is comfortable with the crate, you can offer him his first meal inside it. Leave the door ajar so he can wander in and out as he chooses.

FIRST NIGHT IN HIS NEW HOME

So much has happened in your Swissy puppy's first day away from the breeder. He's had his first car ride to his new home. He's met his new human family and perhaps the other family pets. He has explored his new house and yard, at least those places where he is to be allowed during his first weeks at home. He may have visited his new veterinarian. He has eaten his first meal or two away from his dam and litter-mates. Surely that's enough to tire out an eight-week-old GSMD pup—or so you hope!

It's bedtime. During the day, the pup investigated his crate, which is his new den and sleeping space, so it is not entirely strange to him. Line the crate with a soft towel or blanket that he can snuggle into and gently place him into the crate for the night. Some

breeders send home a piece of bedding from where the pup slept with his littermates, and those familiar scents are a great comfort for the puppy on his first night without his siblings.

He will probably whine or cry. The puppy is objecting to the confinement and the fact that he is alone for the first time. This can be a stressful time for you as well as for the pup. It's important that you remain strong and don't let the puppy out of his crate to comfort him. He will fall asleep eventually. If you release him, the puppy will learn that crying means "out" and will continue

The pup's first day and night in your home can be overwhelming for him. Don't rush the process—let the pup explore while you supervise.

that habit. You are laying the groundwork for future habits. Some breeders find that soft music can soothe a crying pup and help him get to sleep.

SOCIALIZING YOUR PUPPY
The first 20 weeks of your GSMD puppy's life are the most important of his entire lifetime. A properly socialized puppy will grow up to be a confident and stable adult who will be a pleasure to live with and a welcome addition to the neighborhood.

The importance of socialization cannot be overemphasized. Research on canine behavior has proven that puppies who are not exposed to new sights, sounds, people and animals during their first 20 weeks of life will grow up to be timid and fearful, even aggressive, and unable to flourish outside of their home environment.

Socializing your puppy is not difficult and, in fact, will be a fun time for you both. Lead training goes hand in hand with socialization, so your puppy will be learning how to walk on a lead at the same time that he's meeting the neighborhood. Because the Greater Swiss Mountain Dog is such a remarkable breed, everyone will enjoy meeting "the new kid on the block." Take him for short walks to the park and to other dog-friendly places where he will encounter new people, especially children. Puppies automatically recognize children as "little people" and are drawn to play with them. Just make sure that you supervise these meetings and that the children do not get too rough or encourage him to play too hard. An overzealous pup can often nip too hard, frightening the child and in turn making the puppy overly excited. A bad experience in puppyhood can impact a dog for life, so a pup that has a negative experience with a child may grow up to be shy or even aggressive around children.

Take your puppy along on your daily errands. Puppies are natural "people magnets," and most people who see your pup will want to pet him. All of these encounters will help to mold him into a confident adult dog. Likewise, you will soon feel like a confident, responsible dog owner, rightly proud of your mannerly Greater Swiss Mountain Dog.

Be especially careful of your puppy's encounters and experiences during the eight-to-ten-week-old period, which is also called the "fear period." This is a serious imprinting period, and all contact during this time should be gentle and positive. A frightening or negative event could leave a permanent impression that could affect his future behavior if a similar situation arises.

Also make sure that your puppy has received his first and second rounds of vaccinations before you expose him to other dogs or bring him to places that other dogs may frequent. Avoid dog parks and other strange-dog areas until your vet assures you that your puppy is fully immunized and resistant to the diseases that can be passed between canines. Discuss safe early socialization with your breeder and vet, as some recommend socializing the puppy even before he has received all of his inoculations.

LEADER OF THE PUPPY'S PACK
Like other canines, your puppy needs an authority figure,

Your pup will have to adjust to being separated from his siblings, but with love and attention he should settle into his new home nicely.

someone he can look up to and regard as the leader of his "pack." His first pack leader was his dam, who taught him to be polite and not chew too hard on her ears or nip at her muzzle. He learned those same lessons from his litter-mates. If he played too rough, they cried in pain and stopped the game, which sent an important message to the rowdy puppy.

As puppies play together, they are also struggling to determine who will be the boss. Being pack animals, dogs need someone to be in charge. If a litter of puppies remained together beyond puppyhood, one of the pups would emerge as the strongest one, the one who calls the shots.

Once your puppy leaves the pack, he will look intuitively for a new leader. If he does not recognize you as that leader, he will try to assume that position for himself. Of course, it is hard to imagine your adorable Swissy puppy trying to be in charge when he is so small and seemingly helpless. You must remember that these are natural canine instincts and that the Swissy will gladly take over as pack leader if you do not establish yourself in the alpha role. Do not cave in and allow your

BE CONSISTENT

Consistency is a key element, in fact is absolutely necessary, to a puppy's learning environment. A behavior (such as chewing, jumping up or climbing onto the furniture) cannot be forbidden one day and then allowed the next. That will only confuse the pup, and he will not understand what he is supposed to do. Just one or two episodes of allowing an undesirable behavior to "slide" will imprint that behavior on a puppy's brain and make that behavior more difficult to erase or change.

pup to get the upper "paw"!

Just as socialization is so important during these first 20 weeks, so too is your puppy's early education. He was born without any bad habits. He does not know what is good or bad behavior. If he does things like nipping and digging, it's because he is having fun and doesn't know that humans consider these things as "bad." It's your job to teach him proper puppy manners, and this is the best time to accomplish that—before he has developed bad habits, since it is much more difficult to "unlearn" or correct unacceptable learned behavior than to teach good behavior from the start.

Make sure that all members of the family understand the importance of being consistent when training their new puppy. If you tell the puppy to stay off the sofa and your daughter allows him to cuddle on the couch to watch her favorite television show, your pup will be confused about what he is and is not allowed to do. Have a family conference before your pup comes home so that everyone understands the basic principles of puppy training and the rules you have set forth for the pup and agrees to follow them.

The old saying that "an ounce of prevention is worth a pound of cure" is especially true when it comes to puppies. It is much easier to prevent inappropriate behavior than it is to change it. It's also easier and less stressful for the pup, since it will keep discipline to a minimum and create a more positive learning environment for him. That, in turn, will also be easier on you.

Here are a few commonsense tips to keep your belongings safe and your puppy out of trouble:

- Keep your closet doors closed and your shoes, socks and other apparel off the floor so your puppy can't get to them.
- Keep a secure lid on the trash container or put the trash where your puppy can't dig into it. He can't damage what he can't reach.
- Supervise your puppy at all times to make sure he is not getting into mischief. If he starts to chew the corner of the rug, you can distract him instantly by tossing a toy for him to fetch. You also will be able to whisk him outside when you notice that he is about to piddle on the carpet. If you can't see your puppy, you can't teach him or correct his behavior.

SOLVING PUPPY PROBLEMS

CHEWING AND NIPPING

Nipping at fingers and toes is normal puppy behavior. Chewing is also the way that puppies investigate their surroundings. However, you will have to teach your puppy that chewing anything

other than his toys is not acceptable. That won't happen overnight and at times puppy teeth will test your patience. However, if you allow nipping and chewing to continue, just think about the damage that a mature GSMD can do with a full set of adult teeth.

Whenever your puppy nips your hand or fingers, cry out "Ouch!" in a loud voice, which should startle your puppy and stop him from nipping, even if only for a moment. Immediately distract him by offering a small treat or an appropriate toy for him to chew instead (which means having chew toys and puppy treats handy or in your pockets at all times). Praise him when he takes the toy and tell him what a good fellow he is. Praise is just as or even more important in puppy training as discipline and correction.

Keep a watchful eye on your Swissy when outdoors so he isn't getting into anything he shouldn't be.

Puppies also tend to nip at children more often than adults, since they perceive little ones to be more vulnerable and more similar to their littermates. Teach your children appropriate responses to nipping behavior. If they are unable to handle it themselves, you may have to intervene. Puppy nips can be quite painful and a child's frightened reaction will only encourage a puppy to nip harder, which is a natural canine response. As with all other puppy situations, interaction between your Swissy puppy and children should be supervised.

Chewing on objects, not just family members' fingers and ankles, is also normal canine

A teething pup loves soft toys, as chewing them relieves some of the pressure and pain of his aching gums.

THOSE PUPPY TEETH

When a pup is teething and his gums are swollen and sore, wring out a wet face cloth and put it in the freezer. Once frozen, let him chew on it. You can also make logs out of raw hamburger, freeze them and let him enjoy them. A cold raw potato or carrot also helps.

A large raw knucklebone will keep your dog busy for a long time. Never give cooked bones, as they splinter. Do not give thin bones, such as those from a steak. Gnawing on raw bones helps keep the teeth clean and also provides extra calcium, as eventually much of the bone is ground away. The pup may also bury the bone so he can dig it up later, as dogs have done for ages. Look under furniture or under his blanket in his crate where he brings his treasures. You may be surprised at what you find there.

You may find baby teeth here and there in the house. Baby teeth fall out without help, but at times they remain, crowding the permanent teeth. If you see this happening, a visit to the vet is in order. The baby teeth may have to be pulled.

behavior that can be especially tedious (for the owner, not the pup) during the teething period when the puppy's adult teeth are coming in. At this stage, chewing just plain feels good. Furniture legs and cabinet corners are common puppy favorites. Shoes and other personal items also taste pretty good to a pup.

The best solution is, once again, prevention. If you value something, keep it tucked away and out of reach. You can't hide your dining-room table in a closet, but you can try to deflect the chewing by applying a bitter product made just to deter dogs from chewing. This spray-on substance is vile-tasting, although safe for dogs, and most puppies will avoid the forbidden object after one tiny taste. You also can apply the product to your leather leash if the puppy tries to chew on his lead during leash-training sessions.

Keep a ready supply of safe chews handy to offer your Swissy as a distraction when he starts to chew on something that's a "no-no." Remember, at this tender age he does not yet know what is permitted or forbidden, so you have to be "on call" every minute he's awake and on the prowl.

You may lose a treasure or two during puppy's growing-up period, and the furniture could sustain a nasty nick or two. These

Two smiling young Swissys, ready to charm their way into their new owners' hearts.

can be trying times, so be prepared for those inevitable accidents and comfort yourself in knowing that this too shall pass.

PUPPY WHINING
Puppies often cry and whine, just as infants and little children do. It's their way of telling us that they are lonely or in need of attention. Your puppy will miss his littermates and will feel insecure when he is left alone. You may be out of the house or just in another room, but he will still feel alone. During these times, the puppy's crate should be his personal comfort station, a place all his own where he can feel safe and secure. Once he learns that being alone is okay and not something to be feared, he will settle down without crying or objecting. You might want to leave a radio on while he is crated, as the sound of human

voices can be soothing and will give the impression that people are around.

Give your puppy a favorite cuddly toy or chew toy to entertain him whenever he is crated. You will both be happier: the puppy because he is safe in his den and you because he is quiet, safe and not getting into puppy escapades that can wreak havoc in your house or cause him danger.

To make sure that your puppy will always view his crate as a safe and cozy place, never, ever use the crate as punishment. That's the best way to turn the crate into a negative place that the pup will want to avoid. Sure, you can use the crate for your own peace of mind if your puppy is getting into trouble and needs some "time out." Just don't let him know that! Never scold the pup and immediately place him into the crate. Count to ten, give

"People food" can upset your Swissy's diet, add excess weight and even cause him serious illness, so be sure to keep such tantalizing treats out of his reach.

him a couple of hugs and maybe a treat, then scoot him into his crate.

It's also important not to make a big fuss when he is released from the crate. That will make getting out of the crate more appealing than being in the crate, which is just the opposite of what you are trying to achieve.

COUNTER SURFING

What we like to call "counter surfing" is a normal extension of jumping and usually starts to happen as soon as a puppy realizes that he is big enough to stand on his hind legs and investigate the good stuff on the kitchen counter or the coffee table. The Swissy grows into a tall dog, and it won't be long before not much is out of his reach. You therefore have to be there to prevent it. As soon as you see your Swissy even start to raise himself up, startle him with a sharp "No!" or "Aaahh, aaahh!" If he succeeds and manages to get one or both paws on the forbidden surface, smack those paws (firmly but gently) and tell him "Off!" As soon as he's back on all four paws, command him to sit and praise at once.

For surf prevention, make sure to keep any tempting treats or edibles out of reach, where your Swissy can't see or smell them. It's the old rule of prevention yet again.

PROPER CARE OF YOUR

GREATER SWISS MOUNTAIN DOG

Adding a Greater Swiss Mountain Dog to your household means adding a new family member who will need your care each and every day. When your Swissy pup first comes home, you will start a routine with him so that, as he grows up, your dog will have a daily schedule just as you do. The aspects of your dog's daily care will likewise become regular parts of your day, so you'll both have a new schedule. Dogs learn by consistency and thrive on routine: regular times for meals, exercise, grooming and potty trips are just as important for your dog as they are for you. Your dog's schedule will depend much on your family's daily routine, but remember that you now have a new member of the family who is part of your day every day.

FEEDING

Feeding your dog the best diet is based on various factors, including age, activity level, overall condition and size of breed. When you visit the breeder, he will share with you his advice about the proper diet for your dog based on his experience with the breed and the foods with which he has had success. Likewise, your vet will be a helpful source of advice throughout the dog's life and will aid you in planning a diet for optimal health. Proper nutrition and feeding practices are of utmost importance at all stages of a Swissy's life to encourage

Your Greater Swiss puppy depends on you for everything, from his food and water to his education and entertainment.

healthy growth and development as well as to ward off the deadly bloat.

FEEDING THE PUPPY

Of course, your pup's very first food will be his dam's milk. There may be special situations in which pups fail to nurse, necessitating that the breeder hand-feed them with a formula, but for the most part pups spend the first weeks of life nursing from their dam. The breeder weans the pups by gradually introducing solid foods and decreasing the milk meals. Pups may even start themselves off on the weaning process, albeit inadvertently, if they snatch bites from their mom's food bowl.

By the time the pups are ready for new homes, they are fully weaned and eating a good puppy food. As a new owner, you may be thinking, "Great! The breeder has taken care of the hard part." Not so fast.

Although a Swissy continues to develop for his first few years, his first year of life is the time when much of his growth and development takes place. This is a delicate time, and diet plays a huge role in proper skeletal and muscular formation. Improper diet and exercise habits can lead to damaging problems that will compromise the dog's health and movement for his entire life. Since the Swissy is slow to grow

> **SWITCHING FOODS**
> There are certain times in a dog's life when it becomes necessary to switch his food; for example, from puppy to adult food and then from adult to senior-dog food. Additionally, you may decide to feed your pup a different type of food from what he received from the breeder, and there may be "emergency" situations in which you can't find your dog's normal brand and have to offer something else temporarily. Anytime a change is made, for whatever reason, the switch must be done gradually. You don't want to upset the dog's stomach or end up with a picky eater who refuses to eat something new. A tried-and-true approach is, over the course of a few weeks, to mix a little of the new food in with the old, increasing the proportion of new to old as the days progress. In a few weeks, you'll be feeding his regular portions of the new food, and he will barely notice the change.

and mature, avoid a food with too much protein. High protein content stimulates the dog to grow faster, which is rough on the joints. It is unnecessary and, in fact, can prove harmful to add supplements to the diet. Research has shown that too much of certain vitamin supplements and minerals predispose a dog to skeletal problems. It's by no means a case of "if a little is good, a lot is better." At every stage of your dog's life, too much or too little in the way of nutrients can be harmful, which is why a manufactured complete food is the easiest way to know that your dog is getting what he needs.

With so much to consider, new owners should not worry needlessly. With the myriad types of food formulated specifically for growing pups of different-sized breeds, dog-food manufacturers have taken much of the guesswork out of feeding your puppy well. Your breeder also will be an invaluable source of feeding advice. In terms of brands, always feed a premium food and avoid anything with preservatives and other harmful additives. A fish-based food is not recommended.

The exact amount of food to offer a pup depends on the puppy's activity level, weight and the recommendation of your veterinarian. The puppy's breeder can also help you determine how much food is appropriate. Growing puppies generally need proportionately more food per body weight than their adult counterparts, but a pup should never be allowed to gain excess weight. Dogs of all ages should be kept in proper body condition, but extra weight can strain a pup's developing frame, causing skeletal problems.

Regarding the feeding schedule, feeding the pup at the same times and in the same place each day is important for both housebreaking purposes and establishing the dog's everyday routine. Young Swissy puppies need to eat about three or four times a day. Once they get a little older, at about four months old, they can start eating twice a day; this is the schedule on which they should remain for the rest of their lives. Dividing the daily portion into two meals on a morning/evening schedule is much healthier for the dog's digestion than one large daily portion and is considered a preventive measure against bloat.

Watch your pup's weight as he grows and, if the recommended amounts seem to be too much or too little for your pup, consult the vet about appropriate dietary changes. Keep in mind that treats, although small, can quickly add up throughout the day,

Discuss food choices with your breeder. Rely on his experience with the Swissy, and don't stray too far from his and your vet's recommendations.

What Is "Bloat" and How Do I Prevent it?

We have mentioned the term "bloat," which refers to gastric torsion (gastric dilatation/volvulus), a potentially fatal condition. As it is directly related to feeding and exercise practices, a brief explanation here is warranted. The term *dilatation* means that the dog's stomach is filled with air, while *volvulus* means that the stomach is twisted around on itself, blocking the entrance/exit points. Dilatation/volvulus is truly a deadly combination, although they also can occur independently of each other. An affected dog cannot digest food or pass gas, and blood cannot flow to the stomach and other organs, causing accumulation of toxins and gas along with great pain and rapidly occuring shock.

Many theories exist on what exactly causes bloat, but we do know that deep-chested breeds are more prone. Activities like eating a large meal, gulping water, strenuous exercise too close to mealtimes or a combination of these factors can contribute to bloat, though not every case is directly related to these more well-known causes. With that in mind, we can focus on incorporating simple daily preventives and knowing how to recognize the symptoms. In addition to the tips presented in this book, ask your vet about how to prevent and recognize bloat. An affected dog needs immediate veterinary attention, as death can result quickly. Signs include obvious restlessness/discomfort, crying in pain, drooling/excessive salivation, unproductive attempts to vomit or relieve himself, visibly bloated appearance and collapsing. Do not wait: get to the vet *right away* if you see any of these symptoms. The vet will confirm by x-ray if the stomach is bloated with air; if so, the dog must be treated *immediately*.

As varied as the causes of bloat are the tips for prevention, but some common preventive methods follow:
- Feed two or three small meals daily rather than one large one;
- Do not offer water before, after or with meals, but allow access to water at all other times;
- Never permit rapid eating or gulping of water;
- No exercise for the dog at least two hours before and (especially) after meals;
- Feed high-quality food with adequate protein, adequate fiber content and not too much fat and carbohydrate;
- Explore herbal additives, enzymes or gas-reduction products (only under a vet's advice) to encourage a "friendly" environment in the dog's digestive system;
- Avoid foods and ingredients known to produce gas;
- Avoid stressful situations for the dog, especially at mealtimes;
- Make dietary changes gradually, over a period of a few weeks;
- Do not feed dry food only;
- Although the role of genetics as a causative of bloat is not known, many breeders do not breed from previously affected dogs;
- Sometimes owners are advised to have gastropexy (stomach stapling) performed on their dogs as a preventive measure;
- Pay attention to your dog's behavior and any changes that could be symptomatic of bloat. Your dog's life depends on it!

contributing unnecessary calories. Treats are fine when used prudently; opt for dog treats specially formulated to be healthy or for nutritious snacks like small pieces of cheese or cooked chicken.

FEEDING THE ADULT DOG

For the adult (meaning physically mature) dog, feeding properly is about maintenance, not growth. Again, correct weight is a concern. Your dog should appear fit and should have an evident "waist." His ribs should not be protruding (a sign of being underweight), but they should be covered by only a slight layer of fat. Under normal circumstances, an adult dog can be maintained fairly easily with a high-quality, nutritionally complete adult-formula food.

Factor treats into your dog's overall daily caloric intake, and avoid offering table scraps. Not only are some "people foods," like chocolate, nuts, grapes, raisins, onions and large quantities of garlic, toxic to dogs but feeding from your plate also encourages begging and overeating. Overweight dogs are more prone to health problems. Research has even shown that obesity takes years off a dog's life. With that in mind, resist the urge to overfeed and over-treat. Don't make unnecessary additions to your dog's diet, whether with tidbits or with extra vitamins and minerals.

The amount of food needed for proper maintenance will vary depending on the individual dog's activity level, but you will be able to tell whether the daily portions are keeping him in good shape. With the wide variety of good complete foods available, choosing what to feed is largely a matter of personal preference. Just as with the puppy, the adult dog should have consistency in his mealtimes and feeding place; a twice-daily feeding schedule is recommended. In addition to a consistent routine, regular mealtimes allow the Swissy owner to practice the important daily bloat preventives related to

An adult Swissy can be maintained fairly easily on a complete adult-formula food.

years, although he can live longer. (The smallest breeds generally enjoy the longest lives and the largest breeds the shortest.)

What does aging have to do with your dog's diet? No, he won't get a discount at the local diner's early-bird special. Yes, he will require some dietary changes to accommodate the changes that come along with increased age. One change is that the older dog's dietary needs become more similar to that of a puppy. Specifically, a dog's metabolism is different in the puppy, the adult-maintenance and the senior stages of life. Discuss with your vet whether you need to switch to a senior-formulated food or whether your current adult-dog food contains sufficient nutrition for the senior.

Watching the dog's weight remains essential, even more so in the senior stage. Older dogs are already more vulnerable to illness, and obesity only contributes to their susceptibility to problems. As the older dog becomes less active and, thus exercises less, his regular portions may cause him to gain weight. At this point, you may consider decreasing his daily food intake or switching to a reduced-calorie food. As with other changes, you should consult your vet for advice.

Proceed with caution when choosing your Swissy's bowls, as some experts believe that elevated bowls are unwise choices when dealing with deep-chested dogs prone to bloat.

feeding and exercise, such as not allowing exercise for about two hours before and after mealtimes. Regular mealtimes also allow you to see how much your is dog is eating. If the dog seems never to be satisfied or, likewise, becomes uninterested in his food, you will know right away that something is wrong and can consult the vet.

DIETS FOR THE AGING DOG

A good rule of thumb is that once a dog has reached 75% of his expected lifespan, he has reached "senior citizen" or geriatric status. Your Greater Swiss Mountain Dog will be considered a senior at six to seven years of age. Like most large-breed dogs, the Swissy is relatively short-lived; based on his size and breed-specific factors, he has a projected lifespan of eight to ten

THE DARK SIDE OF CHOCOLATE

From a tiny chip to a giant rabbit, chocolate—in any form—is not your dog's friend. Whether it's an Oreo® cookie, a Snickers® bar or even a couple of M&M's®, you should avoid these items with your dog. You are also well advised to avoid any bone toy that is made out of fake chocolate or any treat made of carob—anything that encourages your dog to become a "chocoholic" can't be helpful. Before you toss your pooch half of your candy bar, consider that as little as a single ounce of chocolate can poison a 30-pound dog. Theobromine, like caffeine, is a methylxanthine and occurs naturally in cocoa beans. Dogs metabolize theobromine very slowly, and its effect on the dog can be serious, harming the heart, kidneys and central nervous system. Dark or semi-sweet chocolate is even worse than milk chocolate, and baking chocolate and cocoa mix are by far the worst.

TYPES OF FOOD AND READING THE LABEL

When selecting the type of food to feed your dog, it is important to check out the label for ingredients. Many dry-food products have soybean, corn or rice as the main ingredient. The main ingredient will be listed first on the label, with the rest of the ingredients following in descending order according to their proportion in the food. While these types of dry food are fine, you should look into dry foods based on meat or poultry. These are better-quality foods and thus higher priced. However, they may be just as economical in the long run, because studies have shown that it takes less of the higher-quality foods to maintain a dog.

Comparing the various types of food, dry, canned and semi-moist, dry foods contain the least amount of water and canned foods the most. Proportionately, dry foods are the most calorie- and nutrient-dense, which means that you need more of a canned food product to supply the same amount of nutrition. In households with breeds of disparate sizes, the canned/dry/semi-moist question can be of special importance. Larger breeds obviously eat more than smaller ones and thus in general do better on dry foods, but smaller breeds do fine on canned foods and require "small-bite" formulations to protect their small mouths and teeth if fed dry foods. So if you

The breeder will have started your pup on a quality puppy food and should provide you with feeding instructions so that you can continue a proper diet.

have breeds of different sizes in your household, consider both your own preferences and what your dogs like to eat, but canned food is more appropriate for the little guys and dry or semi-moist for everyone else. You may find success mixing the food types as well. Adding canned food to your Swissy's dry food is recommended to protect against bloat.

There are strict controls that regulate the nutritional content of dog food, and a food has to meet the minimum requirements in order to be considered "complete and balanced." It is important that you choose such a food for your dog, so check the label to be sure that your chosen food meets the requirements. If not, look for a food that clearly states on the label that it is formulated to be complete and balanced for your dog's particular stage of life.

Recommendations for amounts to feed will also be indicated on the label. You should also ask your vet about proper food portions, and you will keep an eye on your dog's condition to see whether the recommended amounts are adequate. If he becomes over- or underweight, you will need to make adjustments; this also would be a good time to consult your vet.

The food label may also make feeding suggestions, such as whether moistening a dry-food product is recommended. Sometimes a splash of water will make the food more palatable for the dog and slow down his eating. Don't be overwhelmed by the

Monitor your Swissy's daily food intake to determine the portions and schedule best for your dog.

many factors that go into feeding your dog. Manufacturers of complete and balanced foods make it easy, and once you find the right food and amounts for your Swissy, his daily feeding will be a matter of routine.

Don't Forget the Water!

Regardless of what type of food he eats, there's no doubt that your Swissy needs plenty of water. Swissys should be well hydrated, especially active puppies and working dogs. Fresh cold water, in a clean bowl, should be made available to your dog. There are special circumstances, such as during puppy housebreaking, when you will want to monitor your pup's water intake so that you will be able to predict when he will need to relieve himself, but water must be available to him nonetheless. Water is essential for hydration and proper body function just as it is for humans.

You will get to know how much your dog typically drinks in a day. Of course, in the heat or if exercising vigorously, he will be more thirsty and will drink more. However, if he begins to drink noticeably more water for no apparent reason, this could signal any of various problems, and you are advised to consult your vet.

A word of caution concerning your deep-chested dog's water intake: he should never be allowed to gulp water, especially at mealtimes. In fact, his water intake should be limited to a few licks at mealtimes as a rule. This simple daily precaution can go a long way in protecting your dog from the dangerous and potentially fatal gastric torsion (bloat).

EXERCISE

We all know the importance of exercise for humans, so it should come as no surprise that it is essential for our canine friends as well. Now, regardless of your own level of fitness, get ready to assume the role of personal trainer for your dog. It's not as hard as it sounds, and it will have health benefits for you, too.

Just as with anything else you do with your dog, you must set a routine for his exercise. It's the same as your daily morning run before work or never missing the

Frolicking about will surely leave your Swissy thirsty. Make sure water is available to him indoors and out.

TWO'S COMPANY

One surefire method of increasing your adult dog's exercise plan is to adopt a second dog. If your dog is well socialized, he should take to his new canine pal in no time and soon the two will be giving each other lots of activity and exercise as they play, romp and explore together. Most owners agree that two dogs are hardly much more work than one. If you cannot afford a second dog, get together with a friend or neighbor who has a well-trained dog. Your dog will definitely enjoy the company of a new four-legged playmate.

7 P.M. aerobics class. If you plan it and get into the habit of actually doing it, it will become just another part of your day. Think of it as making daily exercise appointments with your dog, and stick to your schedule.

As a rule, dogs in normal health should have at least a half-hour of activity each day. Dogs with health or orthopedic problems may have specific limitations, so their exercise plans are best devised with the help of a vet. For healthy dogs, there are many ways to fit 30 minutes of activity into your day. Depending on your schedule, you may plan two 15-minute walks or activity sessions each day or do it all at once in a half-hour session, allowing plenty of time between meals and exercise.

This breed is slow to mature, but once your Swissy is fully developed, you can begin draft training and start to go on long hikes. This is not a "couch potato" breed; Swissys need exercise to remain fit. Games of fetch, long daily walks and

Follow the leader! Initially a puppy received his education and care from his dam. It is now your turn to take over as educator and provider.

general playtime are fine for the pet Swissy. If you want a GSMD that does draft work, you have to build the dog's muscles before you can expect him to pull heavy loads. Long walks and practice with light loads will begin the process.

Some precautions should be taken with a puppy's exercise. Do not vigorously exercise a young GSMD. Before 18 months to 2 years of age, the dog should get most of his exercise from play. If a young Swissy is given too much strenuous exercise too early, there will be damage to the joints. This is not a "jogger's dog" as a puppy or as an adult.

For overweight dogs, dietary changes and activity will help the goal of weight loss. (Sound familiar?) While they should of course be encouraged to be active, remember not to overdo it, as the excess weight is already putting strain on their vital organs and bones. As for highly active dogs, some of them never seem to tire! They will enjoy time spent with their owners doing things together.

Regardless of your dog's condition and activity level, exercise offers benefits to all dogs and owners. Consider the fact that dogs who are kept active are more stimulated both physically and mentally, meaning that they are less likely to become bored and lapse into destructive behavior.

Also consider the benefits of one-on-one time with your dog every day, continually strengthening the bond between the two of you. Furthermore, exercising together will improve health and longevity for both of you. You both need exercise, and now you and your dog have a workout partner and motivator.

GROOMING
Keeping a Swissy clean and smelling good isn't difficult. His short coat is low-maintenance because it is much less oily than that of some other short-haired breeds. The easy coat, combined

Accustom the young puppy to the feel of being brushed. This will make adult grooming sessions easier to manage.

Brushing the Swissy will remove any debris from the coat and keep it looking shiny and clean.

become more extreme for a couple of weeks as the Swissy sheds his undercoat. During this time, the Swissy requires frequent brushing to keep the dead hair from getting all over the carpet and furniture. Even if the hair does get everywhere (which it does), the texture of the Swissy's hair is such that it tends not to stick to fabrics or carpet and is easily vacuumed away.

BATHING

Swissys can go for a very long time between baths without acquiring that "dirty dog" smell. Show dogs may be bathed more frequently, although this depends on the show schedule and the owner. Bathing too frequently can have negative effects on the skin and coat, removing natural oils and causing dryness. When a Swissy must be bathed, though, it is generally an easy task.

If you give your dog his first bath when he is young, he will

WATER SHORTAGE

No matter how well behaved your dog is, bathing is always a project! Nothing can substitute for a good warm bath, but owners do have the option of giving their dogs "dry" baths. Pet shops sell excellent products, in both powder and spray forms, designed for spot-cleaning your dog. These dry shampoos are convenient for touch-up jobs when you don't have the time to bathe your dog in the traditional way.

Muddy feet, messy behinds and smelly coats can be spot-cleaned and deodorized with a "wet-nap"-style cleaner. On those days when your dog insists on rolling in fresh goose droppings and there's no time for a bath, a spot bath can save the day. These pre-moistened wipes are also handy for other grooming needs like wiping faces, ears and eyes and freshening tails and behinds.

with the fact that they are dry-mouthed (no drool!), makes Greater Swiss Mountain Dogs as easy to care for as they are to love.

Swissys rarely need to be bathed. Just brushing a Swissy a few times a week should be adequate to remove loose hair while providing additional opportunities for the owner to bond with his dog and stimulate the dog's coat to be healthy and shiny. However, when the seasons change, especially when winter turns into spring, shedding will

If bathing your Swissy pup outside, only do so in warm weather and make sure to towel him dry.

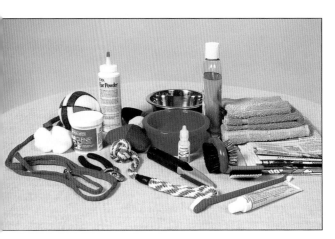

hose or shower spray to wet the coat thoroughly, a few absorbent towels and perhaps a blow dryer.

Before wetting the dog, give him a brush-through to remove any dead hair, dirt and mats. Make sure he is at ease in the tub and have the water at a comfortable temperature. Begin bathing by wetting the coat all the way down to the skin. Massage in the shampoo, keeping it away from his face and eyes. Rinse him thoroughly, again avoiding the eyes and ears, as you don't want to get water into the ear canals. A thorough rinsing is important, as shampoo residue is drying and itchy to the dog. Once the dog is thoroughly rinsed, dry the Swissy completely so he doesn't get a chill. Just towel the dog off, and follow with a hair dryer on a low heat setting in cooler months. Within a few minutes, the Swissy should be dry and smelling fresh. You should keep the dog indoors and away from drafts until he is completely dry.

NAIL CLIPPING

Having their nails trimmed is not on many dogs' lists of favorite things to do. With this in mind, you will need to accustom your puppy to the procedure at a young age so that he will sit still (well, as still as he can) for his pedicures. Long nails can cause the dog's feet to spread, which is not good for him; likewise, long

Your breeder can advise you about the grooming tools you will need for your Swissy. Purchase quality equipment that will withstand frequent use.

become accustomed to the process. Wrestling a dog into the tub or chasing a freshly shampooed dog who has escaped from the bath will be no fun. Most dogs don't naturally enjoy their baths, but you at least want yours to cooperate with you.

Before bathing the dog, have the items you'll need close at hand. First, decide where you will bathe the dog. You should have a tub or basin with a non-slip surface. Young puppies can even be bathed in a sink. In warm weather, some like to use a portable pool in the yard, although you'll want to make sure your dog doesn't head for the nearest dirt pile following his bath! The best kind of shampoo to use is one that is formulated for dogs, one that is gentle on the skin and won't hurt the dog's eyes. Human shampoos are too harsh for dogs' coats and will dry them out. You will also need a

nails can hurt if they unintention-
ally scratch, not good for you!

Some dogs' nails are worn
down naturally by regular walking
on hard surfaces, so the frequency
with which you clip depends on
your individual dog. Look at his
nails from time to time and clip as
needed; a good way to know
when it's time for a trim is if you
hear your dog clicking as he walks
across the floor.

There are several types of nail
clippers and even electric nail-
grinding tools made for dogs; first
we'll discuss using the clipper. To
start, have your clipper ready and
some doggie treats on hand. You
want your pup to view his nail-
clipping sessions in a positive
light, and what better way to
convince him than with food?
You may want to enlist the help
of an assistant to comfort the pup
and offer treats as you concentrate
on the clipping itself. The guillo-
tine-type clipper is thought of by
many as the easiest type to use;
the nail tip is inserted into the
opening, and blades on the top
and bottom snip it off in one clip.

Start by grasping the pup's
paw; a little pressure on the foot
pad causes the nail to extend,
making it easier to clip. Clip off a
little at a time. If you can see the
"quick," which is a blood vessel
that runs through each nail, you
will know how much to trim, as
you do not want to cut into the
quick. On that note, if you do cut

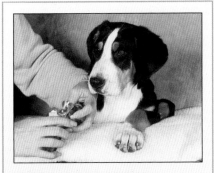

THE MONTHLY GRIND

If your dog doesn't like the feeling of
nail clippers or if you're not
comfortable using them, you may
wish to try an electric nail grinder.
This tool has a small sandpaper disc
on the end that rotates to grind the
nails down. Some feel that using a
grinder reduces the risk of cutting
into the quick; this can be true if the
tool is used properly. Usually you will
be able to tell where the quick is
before you get to it. A benefit of the
grinder is that it creates a smooth
finish on the nails so that there are no
ragged edges.

Because the tool makes noise, your
dog should be introduced to it before
the actual grinding takes place. Turn it
on and let your dog hear the noise;
turn it off and let him inspect it with
you holding it. Use the grinder gently,
holding it firmly and progressing a
little at a time until you reach the
proper length. Look at the nail as you
grind so that you do not go too short.
Stop at any indication that you are
nearing the quick. It will take a few
sessions for both you and the puppy
to get used to the grinder.

If you introduce your Greater Swiss puppy to the nail-clipping routine, you will be blessed with an adult who doesn't mind having his regular pedicures.

cue to stop clipping. Tell the puppy he's a "good boy" and offer a piece of treat with each nail. You can also use nail-clipping time to examine the footpads, making sure that they are not dry and cracked and that nothing has become embedded in them.

The nail grinder, the other choice, is many owners' first choice. Accustoming the puppy to the sound of the grinder and sensation of the buzz presents fewer challenges than the clipper, and there's no chance of cutting through the quick. Use the grinder on a low setting and always talk soothingly to your dog. He won't mind his salon visit, and he'll have nicely polished nails as well.

EAR CLEANING

While keeping your dog's ears clean unfortunately will not cause him to "hear" your commands any better, it will protect him from ear infection and ear-mite infestation. In addition, a dog's ears are vulnerable to waxy build-up and to collecting foreign matter from the outdoors. Look in your dog's ears regularly to ensure that they look pink, clean and otherwise healthy. Even if they look fine, an odor in the ears signals a problem and means it's time to call the vet.

the quick, which will cause bleeding, you can stem the flow of blood with a styptic pencil or other clotting agent. If you mistakenly nip the quick, do not panic or fuss, as this will cause the pup to be afraid. Simply reassure the pup, stop the bleeding and move on to the next nail. Don't be discouraged; you will become a professional canine pedicurist with practice.

You may or may not be able to see the quick, so it's best to just clip off a small bit at a time. If you see a dark dot in the center of the nail, this is the quick and your

A dog's ears should be cleaned regularly; once a week is suggested, and you can do this along with your regular brushing.

Using a cotton ball or pad and never probing into the ear canal, wipe the ear gently. You can use an ear-cleansing liquid or powder available from your vet or pet-supply store; alternatively, you might prefer to use homemade solutions with ingredients like white vinegar or hydrogen peroxide. Ask your vet about home remedies before you attempt to concoct something on your own!

Keep your dog's ears free of excess hair by plucking it as needed. If done gently, this will be painless for the dog. Look for wax, brown droppings (a sign of ear mites), redness or any other abnormalities. At the first sign of a problem, contact your vet so that he can prescribe an appropriate medication.

EYE CARE
During grooming sessions, pay extra attention to the condition of your dog's eyes. If the area around the eyes is soiled or if tear staining has occurred, there are

THE EARS KNOW
Examining your puppy's ears helps ensure good internal health. The ears are the eyes to the dog's innards! Begin handling your puppy's ears when he's still young so that he doesn't protest every time you lift a flap or touch his ears. Yeast and bacteria are two of the culprits that you can detect by examining the ear. You will notice a strong, often foul, odor, debris, redness or some kind of discharge. All of these point to health problems that can worsen over time. Additionally, you are on the lookout for wax accumulation, ear mites and other tiny bothersome parasites and their even tinier droppings. You may have to pluck hair with tweezers in order to have a better view into the dog's ears, but this is painless if done carefully.

When cleaning your dog's ears, it is best to use cotton balls instead of cotton swabs (shown here), which could harm the dog's inner ear.

various cleaning agents made especially for this purpose. Look at the dog's eyes to make sure no debris has entered; dogs with large eyes and those who spend time outdoors are especially prone to this.

The signs of an eye infection are obvious: mucus, redness, puffiness, scabs or other signs of irritation. If your dog's eyes become infected, the vet will likely prescribe an antibiotic ointment for treatment. If you notice signs of more serious problems, such as opacities in the eye, which usually indicate cataracts, consult the vet at once. Taking time to pay attention to your dog's eyes will alert you in the early stages of any problem so that you can get your dog treatment as soon as possible. You could save your dog's sight.

A Swissy flashing his pearly whites! Crunchy food and treats are good for a dog's dental health, as the hard particles help scrape away plaque as the dog chews.

A CLEAN SMILE

Another essential part of grooming is brushing your dog's teeth and checking his overall oral condition. Studies show that around 80% of dogs experience dental problems by two years of age, and the percentage is higher in older dogs. Therefore it is highly likely that your dog will have trouble with his teeth and gums unless you are proactive with home dental care.

The most common dental problem in dogs is plaque build-up. If not treated, this causes gum disease, infection and resultant tooth loss. Bacteria from these infections spread throughout the body, affecting the vital organs. Do you need much more convincing to start brushing your dog's teeth? If so, take a good whiff of your dog's breath, and read on.

Fortunately, home dental care is rather easy and convenient for pet owners. Specially formulated

As with other grooming tasks, accustom your Swissy pup to his dental care early on. Start gently, for a few minutes at a time, so that he gets used to the feel of the brush and to your handling his mouth. Offer praise and petting so that he looks at tooth-care time as a time when he gets extra love and attention. The routine should become second nature; he may not like it, but he should at least tolerate it.

Aside from brushing, offer dental toys to your dog and feed crunchy biscuits, which help to minimize plaque. Rope toys have the added benefit of acting like floss as the dog chews. At your adult dog's yearly check-ups, the vet will likely perform a thorough

It is important to keep the eye area clean. This can be done easily with a soft wipe and either warm water or a cleansing solution made for this purpose.

canine toothpaste is easy to find. You should use one of these toothpastes, not a product for humans. Some doggie pastes are even available in flavors appealing to dogs. If your dog likes the flavor, he will tolerate the process better, making things much easier for you. Doggie toothbrushes come in different sizes and are designed to fit the contour of a canine mouth. Rubber fingertip brushes fit right on one of your fingers and have rubber nodes to clean the teeth and massage the gums. This may be easier to handle, as it is akin to rubbing your dog's teeth with your finger.

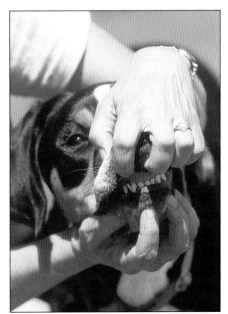

Toothbrushing and regular mouth inspections are part of your Swissy's home-care routine. Specially made doggie toothbrushes and paste are available from your vet or pet-supply store.

tooth scraping as well as a complete check for any problems. Proper care of your dog's teeth will ensure that you will enjoy your dog's smile for many years to come. The next time your dog goes to give you a hello kiss, you'll be glad you spent the time caring for his teeth.

THE OTHER END

Dogs sometime have troubles with their anal glands, which are sacs located beside the anal vent. These should empty when a dog has normal bowel movements; if they don't, they can become full or impacted, causing discomfort. Owners often are alarmed to see their dogs scooting across the floor, dragging their behinds behind, this is just a dog's attempt to empty the glands himself.

Some brave owners attempt to evacuate their dogs' anal glands themselves during grooming, but no one will tell you that this is a

PET OR STRAY?
Besides the obvious benefit of providing your contact information to whoever finds your lost dog, an ID tag makes your dog more approachable and more likely to be recovered. A strange dog wandering the neighborhood without a collar and tags will look like a stray, while the collar and tags indicate that the dog is someone's pet. Even if the ID tags become detached from the collar, the collar alone will make a person more likely to pick up the dog.

pleasant task. Thus many owners prefer to make the trip to the vet to have the vet take care of the problem; owners whose dogs visit a groomer can have this done by the groomer if he offers this as part of his services. Regardless, don't neglect the dog's other end in your home-care routine. Look for scooting, licking or other signs of discomfort "back there" to ascertain whether the anal glands need to be emptied.

IDENTIFICATION FOR YOUR DOG

You love your Greater Swiss Mountain Dog and want to keep him safe. Of course you take every precaution to prevent his escaping from the yard or becoming lost or stolen. You have a sturdy high fence and you always keep your dog on lead when out and about

No dog should ever be without his identification tags, which should be securely attached to his everyday collar.

in public places. If your dog is not properly identified, however, you are overlooking a major aspect of his safety. We hope to never be in a situation where our dog is missing, but we should practice prevention in the unfortunate case that this happens; identification greatly increases the chances of your dog's being returned to you.

There are several ways to identify your dog. First, the traditional dog tag should be a staple in your dog's wardrobe, attached to his everyday collar. Tags can be made of sturdy plastic and various metals and should include your contact information so that a person who finds the dog can get in touch with you right away to arrange his return. Many people today enjoy the wide range of decorative tags available, so have fun and create a tag to match your dog's personality. Of course, it is important that the tag stays on the collar, so have a secure "O"-ring attachment; you also can explore the type of tag that slides right onto the collar.

In addition to the ID tag, which every dog should wear even if identified by another method, two other forms of identification have become popular: microchipping and tattooing. In microchipping, a tiny scannable chip is painlessly inserted under the dog's skin. The number is registered to you so that, if your lost dog turns up at a clinic or

shelter, the chip can be scanned to retrieve your contact information.

The advantage of the microchip is that it is a permanent form of ID, but there are some factors to consider. Several different companies make microchips, and not all are compatible with the others' scanning devices. It's best to find a company with a universal microchip that can be read by scanners made by other companies as well. It won't do any good to have the dog chipped if the information cannot be retrieved. Also, not every humane society, shelter and clinic is equipped with a scanner, although more and more facilities are equipping themselves. In fact, many shelters microchip dogs that they adopt out to new homes.

In the US, there are five or six major microchip manufacturers as well as a few databases, such as HomeAgain™ Companion Animal Retrieval System (Schering-Plough) and

Your pet Swissys should wear their identification at all times, even when spending time in an enclosed yard.

the American Kennel Club's Companion Animal Recovery Unit.

Because the microchip is not visible to the eye, the dog must wear a tag that states that he is microchipped so that whoever picks him up will know to have him scanned. This tag usually also indicates the registry's phone number and the dog's microchip ID number. He of course also should have a tag with your contact information in case his information cannot be retrieved. Humane societies and veterinary clinics offer microchipping service, which is usually very affordable.

Though less popular than microchipping, tattooing is another permanent method of ID for dogs. Most vets perform this service, and there are also clinics that perform dog tattooing. This is also an affordable procedure and one that will not cause much discomfort for the dog. It is best to put the tattoo in a visible area, such as the ear, to deter theft. It is sad to say that there are cases of dogs' being stolen and sold to research laboratories, but such laboratories will not accept tattooed dogs.

To ensure that the tattoo is effective in aiding your dog's return to you, the tattoo number must be registered with a national organization. That way, when someone finds a tattooed dog, a phone call to the registry will quickly match the dog with his owner.

BOARDING

Today there are many options for dog owners who need someone to care for their dogs in certain circumstances. While many think of boarding their dogs as something to do when away on vacation, many others use the services of doggie "daycare" facilities, dropping their dogs off to spend the day while they are at work. Many of these facilities offer both long-term and daily care. Many go beyond just boarding and cater to all sorts of needs, with on-site grooming, veterinary care, training classes and even "web-cams" where owners can log onto the Internet and check out what their dogs are up to. Most dogs enjoy the activity and time spent with other dogs.

Before you need to use such a service, check out the ones in your area. Make visits to see the facilities, meet the staff, discuss fees and available services and see whether this is a place where you think your dog will be happy. It is best to do your research in advance so that you're not stuck at the last minute, forced into making a rushed decision without knowing whether the kennel that you've chosen meets your standards. You also can check with your vet's office to see whether they offer boarding for their clients or can recommend a good kennel in the area.

The kennel will need to see proof of your dog's health records and vaccinations so as not to spread illness from dog to dog. Your dog also will need proper identification. Owners usually experience some separation anxiety the first time they have to leave their dog in someone else's care, so it's reassuring to know that the kennel you choose is run by experienced, caring, true dog people.

Do your research ahead of time if you need to board your dog. You want to be totally comfortable with the facility you choose.

GREATER SWISS MOUNTAIN DOG

BASIC TRAINING PRINCIPLES: PUPPY VS. ADULT

There's a big difference between training an adult dog and training a young puppy. With a young puppy, everything is new! At eight to ten weeks of age, he will be experiencing many things, and he has nothing with which to compare these experiences. Up to this point, he has been with his dam and littermates, not one-on-one with people except in his interactions with his breeder and visitors to the litter.

When you first bring the

Training forms the basis of a rewarding and fulfilling relationship with your four-legged family member.

puppy home, he is eager to please you. This means that he accepts doing things your way. During the next couple of months, he will absorb the basis of everything he needs to know for the rest of his life. This early age is even referred to as the "sponge" stage. After that, for the next 18 months, it's up to you to reinforce good manners by building on the foundation that you've established. Once your puppy is reliable in basic commands and behavior and has reached the appropriate age, you may gradually introduce him to some of the interesting sports, games and activities available to pet owners and their dogs.

Raising your puppy is a family affair. Each member of the family must know what rules to set forth for the puppy and how to use the same one-word commands to mean exactly the same thing every time. Even if yours is a large family, one person will soon be considered by the pup to be the leader, the alpha person in his pack, the "boss" who must be obeyed. Often that highly regarded person turns out to be the one who feeds the puppy. Food ranks very high on the puppy's list of important things. That's why your puppy is rewarded with small treats along with verbal praise when he responds to you correctly. As the puppy learns to do what you want him to do, the food rewards are gradually eliminated and only the praise remains. If you were to keep up with the food treats, you could have two problems on your hands—an obese dog and a beggar.

Training begins the minute your Swissy puppy steps through the doorway of your home, so don't make the mistake of putting the puppy on the floor and telling him by your actions to "Go for it! Run wild!" Even if this is your first puppy, you must act as if you know what you're doing: be the boss. An uncertain pup may be terrified to move, while a bold one will be ready to take you at your word and start plotting to destroy the house! Before you collected your puppy, you decided where his own special place would be, and that's where to put him when you first arrive home. Give him a house tour after he has investigated his area and had a nap and a bathroom "pit stop."

It's worth mentioning here that if you've adopted an adult dog that is completely trained to your liking, lucky you! You're off the hook! However, if that dog

spent his life up to this point in a kennel, or even in a good home but without any real training, be prepared to tackle the job ahead. A dog three years of age or older with no previous training cannot be blamed for not knowing what

Puppies start out life as a clean slate—no bad habits! It's up to you to mold your pup's behavior and nurture a well-mannered canine citizen.

THE RIGHT START
The best advice for a potential dog owner is to start with the very best puppy that money can buy. Don't shop around for a bargain in the newspaper. You're buying a companion, not a used car or a second-hand appliance. The purchase price of the dog represents a very significant part of the investment, but this is indeed a very small sum compared to the expenses of maintaining the dog in good health. If you purchase a well-bred, healthy and sound puppy, you will be starting right. An unhealthy puppy can cost you thousands of dollars in unnecessary veterinary expenses and, possibly, a fortune in heartbreak as well.

he was never taught. While the dog is trying to understand and learn your rules, at the same time he has to unlearn many of his previously self-taught habits and general view of the world.

Working with a professional trainer will speed up your progress with an adopted adult dog. You'll need patience, too. Some new rules may be close to impossible for the dog to accept. After all, he's been successful so far by doing everything his way! (Patience again.) He may agree with your instruction for a few days and then slip back into his old ways, so you must be just as consistent and understanding in your teaching as you would be with a puppy. (More patience needed yet again!) Your dog has to learn to pay attention to your voice, your family, the daily routine, new smells, new sounds and, in some cases, even a new climate.

One of the most important things to find out about a newly adopted adult dog is his reaction to children (yours and others), strangers and your friends, and how he acts upon meeting other dogs. If he was not socialized with dogs as a puppy, this could be a major problem. This does not mean that he's a "bad" dog, a vicious dog or an aggressive dog; rather, it means that he has no idea how to read another dog's body language. There's no way for him to tell whether the other dog is a friend or foe. Survival instinct takes over, telling him to attack first and ask questions later. This

---

DAILY SCHEDULE

How many relief trips does your puppy need per day? A puppy up to the age of 14 weeks will need to go outside about 8 to 12 times per day! You will have to take the pup out any time he starts sniffing around the floor or turning in small circles, as well as after naps, meals, games and lessons or whenever he's released from his crate. Once the puppy is 14 to 22 weeks of age, he will require only 6 to 8 relief trips. At the ages of 22 to 32 weeks, the puppy will require about 5 to 7 trips. Adult dogs typically require 4 relief trips per day, in the morning, afternoon, evening and late at night.

You can start out with paper-training your young Swissy pup, but outdoor toilet training is the best option for this large breed.

definitely calls for professional help and, even then, may not be a behavior that can be corrected 100% reliably (or even at all). If you have a puppy, this is why it is so very important to introduce your young puppy properly to other puppies and "dog-friendly" adult dogs.

HOUSE-TRAINING YOUR GSMD
Dogs are tactility-oriented when it comes to house-training. In other words, they respond to the surface on which they are given approval to eliminate. The choice is yours (the dog's version is in parentheses): The lawn (including the neighbors' lawns)? A bare patch of earth under a tree (where people like to sit and relax in the summertime)? Concrete steps or patio (all sidewalks, garages and basement floors)? The curbside (watch out for cars)? A small area of crushed stone in a corner of the yard (mine!)? The latter is the best choice if you can manage it, because it will remain strictly for the dog's use and is easy to keep clean.

You can start out with paper-training indoors and switch over to an outdoor surface as the puppy matures and gains control over his need to eliminate. For the naysayers, don't worry—this won't mean that the dog will soil on every piece of newspaper lying around the house. You are training him to go outside, remember? Starting out by paper-training often is the only choice for a city dog.

old, the puppy will have to be taken outside every time he wakes up, about 10–15 minutes after every meal and after every period of play—all day long, from first thing in the morning until his bedtime! That's a total of ten or more trips per day to teach the puppy where it's okay to relieve himself. With that schedule in mind, you can see that house-training a young puppy is not a part-time job. It requires someone to be home all day.

If that seems overwhelming or impossible, do a little planning. For example, plan to pick up your puppy at the start of a vacation period. If you can't get home in the middle of the day, plan to hire a dog-sitter or ask a neighbor to come over to take the pup outside, feed him his lunch and then take him out again about ten or so minutes after he's eaten. Also make arrangements with that or another person to be your "emergency" contact if you have to stay late on the job. Remind yourself—repeatedly—that this hectic schedule improves as the puppy gets older.

HOME WITHIN A HOME

Your GSMD puppy needs to be confined to one secure, puppy-proof area when no one is able to watch his every move. Generally, the kitchen is the place of choice because the floor is washable. Likewise, it's a busy family area

TIDY BOY

Clean by nature, dogs do not like to soil their dens, which in effect are their crates or sleeping quarters. Unless not feeling well, dogs will not defecate or urinate in their crates. Crate training capitalizes on the dog's natural desire to keep his den clean. Be conscientious about giving the puppy as many opportunities to relieve himself outdoors as possible. Reward the puppy for correct behavior. Praise him and pat him whenever he "goes" in the correct location. Even the tidiest of puppies can have potty accidents, so be patient and dedicate more energy to helping your puppy achieve a clean lifestyle.

WHEN YOUR PUPPY'S "GOT TO GO"

Your puppy's need to relieve himself is seemingly non-stop, but signs of improvement will be seen each week. From 8 to 10 weeks that will accustom the pup to a variety of noises, everything from pots and pans to the telephone, blender and dishwasher. He will also be enchanted by the smell of your cooking (and will never be critical when you burn something). An exercise pen (also called an "ex-pen," a puppy version of a playpen) within the room of choice can help as a means of confinement for a young pup. He can see out and has a certain amount of space in which to run about, but he is safe from dangerous things like electrical cords, heating units, trash baskets or open kitchen-supply cabinets. Place the pen where the puppy will not get a blast of heat or air conditioning.

In the pen, you can put a few toys, his bed (which can be his crate if the dimensions of pen and crate are compatible) and a few layers of newspaper in one small corner, just in case. A water bowl can be hung at a convenient height on the side of the ex-pen so it won't become a splashing pool for an innovative puppy. His food dish can go on the floor, near but not under the water bowl.

Crates are something that pet owners are at last getting used to for their dogs. Wild or domestic canines have always preferred to sleep in den-like safe spots, and that is exactly what the crate provides. How often have you seen adult dogs that choose to

sleep under a table or chair even though they have full run of the house? It's the den connection.

In your "happy" voice, use the word "Crate" every time you put the pup into his den. If he's new to a crate, toss in a small biscuit for him to chase the first few times. At night, after he's been outside, he should sleep in his crate. The crate may be kept in his designated area at night or, if you want to be sure to hear those wake-up yips in the morning, put the crate in a corner of your bedroom. However, don't make any response whatsoever to whining or crying. If he's completely ignored, he'll settle down and get to sleep.

Good bedding for a young puppy is an old folded bath towel or an old blanket, something that is easily washable and disposable if necessary ("accidents" will happen!). Never put newspaper in the puppy's crate. Also those old

Scent attraction will lead your pup to his proper bathroom area.

POTTY COMMAND

Most dogs love to please their masters; there are no bounds to what dogs will do to make their owners happy. The potty command is a good example of this theory. If toileting on command makes the master happy, then more power to him. Puppies will obligingly piddle if it really makes their keepers smile. Some owners can be creative about which word they will use to command their dogs to relieve themselves. Some popular choices are "Potty," "Tinkle," "Piddle," "Let's go," "Hurry up" and "Toilet." Give the command every time your puppy goes into position and the puppy will begin to associate his business with the command.

of being chewed to bits. Squeaky parts, bits of stuffing or plastic or any other small pieces can cause intestinal blockage or possibly choking if swallowed.

PROGRESSING WITH POTTY-TRAINING

After you've taken your puppy out and he has relieved himself in the area you've selected, he can have some free time with the family as long as there is someone responsible for watching him. That doesn't mean just someone in the same room who is watching TV or busy on the computer but one person who is doing nothing other than keeping an eye on the pup, playing with him on the floor and helping him understand his position in the pack.

This first taste of freedom will let you begin to set the house rules. If you don't want the dog on the furniture, now is the time to prevent his first attempts to jump up onto the couch. The word to use in this case is "Off," not "Down." "Down" is the word you will use to teach the down position, which is something entirely different.

Most corrections at this stage come in the form of simply distracting the puppy. Instead of telling him "No" for "Don't chew the carpet," distract the chomping puppy with a toy and he'll forget about the carpet.

As you are playing with the pup, do not forget to watch him

ideas about adding a clock to replace his mother's heartbeat or a hot-water bottle to replace her warmth, are just that—old ideas. The clock could drive the puppy nuts, and the hot-water bottle could end up as a very soggy waterbed! An extremely good breeder would have introduced your puppy to the crate by letting two pups sleep together for a couple of nights, followed by several nights alone. How thankful you will be if you found that breeder!

Safe toys in the pup's crate or area will keep him occupied, but monitor their condition closely. Discard any toys that show signs closely and pay attention to his body language. Whenever you see him begin to circle or sniff, take the puppy outside to relieve himself. If you are paper-training, put him back into his confined area on the newspapers. In either case, praise him as he eliminates while he actually is in the act of relieving himself. Three seconds after he has finished is too late. You'll be praising him for running toward you, picking up a toy or whatever he may be doing at that moment, and that's not what you want to be praising him for. Timing is a vital tool in all dog training. Use it.

Remove soiled newspapers immediately and replace them with clean ones. You may want to take a small piece of soiled paper and place it in the middle of the new clean papers, as the scent will attract him to that spot when it's time to go again. That scent attraction is why it's so important to clean up any messes made in the house by using a product specially made to eliminate the odor of dog urine and droppings. Regular household cleansers won't do the trick. Pet shops sell the best pet deodorizers. Invest in the largest container you can find.

Scent attraction eventually will lead your pup to his chosen spot outdoors; this is the basis of outdoor training. When you take your puppy outside to relieve himself, use a one-word command such as "Outside" or "Go-potty" (that's one word to the puppy!) as you attach his leash. Then quickly lead him to his spot. Now comes the hard part—hard for you, that is. Just stand there until he urinates and defecates. Move him a few feet in one direction or another if he's just sitting there looking at you, but remember that this is neither playtime nor time for a walk. This is strictly a business trip. Then, as he circles and squats (remember your timing), give him a quiet "Good dog" as praise. If you start to jump for joy, ecstatic over his performance, he'll do one of two things: either he will stop mid-stream, as it were, or he'll do it again for you—in the house—and expect you to be just as delighted.

Give him five minutes or so and, if he doesn't go in that time, take him back indoors to his confined area and try again in another ten minutes, or immedi-

The timing of your reward is essential. Make sure your pup knows he's being rewarded for going to the bathroom in the correct location.

ately if you see him sniffing and circling. By careful observation, you'll soon work out a successful schedule.

Accidents, by the way, are just that—accidents. Clean them up quickly and thoroughly, without comment, after the puppy has been taken outside to finish his business and then put back into his area or crate. If you witness an accident in progress, say "No!" in a stern voice and get the pup outdoors immediately. No punishment is needed. You and your puppy are just learning each other's language, and sometimes it's easy to miss a puppy's message. Chalk it up to experience and watch more closely from now on.

Swissys are affectionate dogs that love to spend time with their owners. Training furthers the communication and bond between dog and owner.

SMILE WHEN YOU ORDER ME AROUND!

While trainers recommend practicing with your dog every day, it's perfectly acceptable to take a "mental health day" off. It's better not to train the dog on days when you're in a sour mood. Your bad attitude or lack of interest will be sensed by your dog, and he will respond accordingly. Studies show that dogs are well tuned in to their humans' emotions. Be conscious of how you use your voice when talking to your dog. Raising your voice or shouting will only erode your dog's trust in you as his trainer and master.

KEEPING THE PACK ORDERLY

Discipline is a form of training that brings order to life. For example, military discipline is what allows the soldiers in an army to work as one. Discipline is a form of teaching and, in dogs, is the basis of how the successful pack operates. Each member knows his place in the pack and all respect the leader, or alpha dog. It is essential for your puppy that you establish this type of relationship, with you as the alpha, or leader. It is a form of social coexistence that all canines recognize and accept. Discipline, therefore, is never to be confused with punishment. When you teach your puppy how you want him to behave, and he behaves properly and you praise him for it, you are disciplining him with a form of positive reinforcement.

For a dog, rewards come in the form of praise, a smile, a cheerful tone of voice, a few friendly pats or a rub of the ears. Rewards are also small food treats. Obviously, that does not mean bits of regular dog food. Instead, treats are very small bits of special things like cheese or pieces of soft dog treats. The idea is to reward the dog with something very small that he can taste and swallow, providing instant positive reinforcement. If he has to take time to chew the treat, by the time he is finished he will have forgotten what he did to earn it.

Your puppy should never be physically punished. The displeasure shown on your face and in your voice is sufficient to signal to the pup that he has done something wrong. He wants to please everyone higher up on the social ladder, especially his leader, so a scowl and harsh voice will take care of the error. Growling out the word "Shame!" when the pup is caught in the act of doing something wrong is better than the repetitive "No." Some dogs hear "No" so often that they begin to think it's their name! By the way, do not use the dog's name when you're correcting him. His name is reserved to get his attention for something pleasant about to take place.

There are punishments that have nothing to do with you. For example, your dog may think that chasing cats is one reason for his existence. You can try to stop it as much as you like but without success, because it's such fun for the dog. But one good hissing, spitting swipe of a cat's claws across the dog's nose will put an end to the game forever. Intervene only when your dog's eyeball is seriously at risk. Cat scratches can cause permanent damage to an innocent but annoying puppy.

Always let your Swissy know when he's done his job well; he thrives on your approval and praise.

The result of a properly trained Swissy will be a dog that is easy to care for and even easier to love.

PUPPY KINDERGARTEN

COLLAR AND LEASH

Before you begin your GSMD puppy's education, he must be used to his collar and leash. Choose a collar for your puppy that is secure, but not heavy or bulky. He won't enjoy training if he's uncomfortable. A flat buckle collar is fine for everyday wear and for initial puppy training. For older dogs, there are several types of training collars such as the martingale, which is a double loop that tightens slightly around the neck, or the head collar, which is similar to a horse's halter. A chain choke collar is not a recommended training tool for your GSMD.

A lightweight 6-foot woven cotton or nylon training leash is preferred by most trainers because it is easy to fold up in your hand and comfortable to hold because there is a certain amount of give to it. There are lessons where the dog will start off 6 feet away from you at the end of the leash. The leash used to take the puppy outside to relieve himself is shorter because you don't want him to roam away from his area. The shorter leash will also be the one to use when you walk the puppy.

LEASH TRAINING

House-training and leash training go hand in hand, literally. When taking your puppy outside to do his business, lead him there on his leash. Unless an emergency potty run is called for, do not whisk the puppy up into your arms and take him outside. If you have a fenced yard, you have the advantage of letting the puppy loose to go out, but it's better to put the dog on the leash and take him to his designated place in the yard until he is reliably house-trained. Taking the puppy for a walk is the best way to house-train a dog. The dog will associate the walk with his time to relieve himself, and the exercise of walking stimulates the dog's bowels and bladder. Dogs that are not trained to relieve themselves on a walk may hold it until they get back home, which of course defeats half the purpose of the walk.

If you've been wise enough to enroll in a puppy kindergarten training class, suggestions will be made as to the best collar and leash for your young puppy. I say "wise" because your puppy will be in a class with puppies in his age range (up to five months old) of all breeds and sizes. It's the perfect way for him to learn the right way (and the wrong way) to interact with other dogs as well as their people. You cannot teach your puppy how to interpret another dog's sign language. For a first-time puppy owner, these socialization classes are invaluable. For experienced dog owners, they are a real boon to further training.

ATTENTION

You've been using the dog's name since the minute you collected him from the breeder, so you should be able to get his attention by saying his name—with a big smile and in an excited tone of voice. His response will be the puppy equivalent of "Here I am! What are we going to do?" Your immediate response (if you haven't guessed by now) is "Good dog." Rewarding him at the moment he pays attention to you teaches him the proper way to respond when he hears his name.

EXERCISES FOR A BASIC CANINE EDUCATION

THE SIT EXERCISE

There are several ways to teach the puppy to sit. The first one is to catch him whenever he is about to sit and, as his backside nears the floor, say "Sit, good dog!" That's positive reinforcement and, if your timing is sharp, he will learn that what he's doing at that second is connected to your saying "Sit" and that you think he's clever for doing it!

Another method is to start with the puppy on his leash in front of you. Show him a treat in the palm of your right hand. Bring your hand up under his nose and, almost in slow motion, move your hand up and back so his nose goes up in the air and his head

Once the sit command is learned, practice it at the beginning and end of every lesson. Success builds confidence in your Swissy pupil.

Praise and a tasty morsel are the keys to the Swissy's kingdom—and the keys to your training success.

of the hand are signals for the sit. Your puppy is watching you almost more than he is listening to you, so what you do is just as important as what you say.

Don't save any of these drills only for training sessions. Use them as much as possible at odd times during a normal day. The dog should always sit before being given his food dish. He should sit to let you go through a doorway first, when the doorbell rings or when you stop to speak to someone on the street.

THE DOWN EXERCISE

Before beginning to teach the down command, you must consider how the dog feels about this exercise. To him, "down" is a submissive position. Being flat on the floor with you standing over him is not his idea of fun. It's up

tilts back as he follows the treat in your hand. At that point, he will have to either sit or fall over, so as his back legs buckle under, say "Sit, good dog," and then give him the treat and lots of praise. You may have to begin with your hand lightly running up his chest, actually lifting his chin up until he sits. Some (usually older) dogs require gentle pressure on their hindquarters with the left hand, in which case the dog should be on your left side. Puppies generally do not appreciate this physical dominance.

After a few times, you should be able to show the dog a treat in the open palm of your hand, raise your hand waist-high as you say "Sit" and have him sit. You thereby have taught him two things at the same time. Both the verbal command and the motion

DOWN

"Down" is a harsh-sounding word and a submissive posture in dog body language, thus presenting two obstacles in teaching the down command. When the dog is about to flop down on his own, tell him "Good down." Pups that are not good about being handled learn better by having food lowered in front of them. A dog that trusts you can be gently guided into position. When you give the command "Down," be sure to say it sweetly!

lunge for the food. As the puppy goes into the down position, say "Down" very gently.

The difficulty with this exercise is twofold: it's both the submissive aspect and the fact that most people say the word "Down" as if they were drill sergeants in charge of recruits! So issue the command sweetly, give him the treat and have the pup maintain the down position for several seconds. If he tries to get up immediately, place your hands on his shoulders and press down gently, giving him a very quiet "Good dog." As you progress with this lesson, increase the "down time" until he will hold it until you say "Okay" (his cue for release). Practice this one in the house at various times throughout the day.

By increasing the length of time during which the dog must maintain the down position, you'll find many uses for it. For example, he can lie at your feet in the vet's office or anywhere that both of you have to wait, when you are on the phone, while the family is eating and so forth. If you progress to training for competitive obedience, he'll already be all set for the exercise called the "long down."

THE STAY EXERCISE
You can teach your Swissy to stay in the sit, down and stand positions. To teach the sit/stay,

If training outside, especially in the warm summer months, be sure to take frequent breathers that allow the puppy to rest and re-hydrate with some fresh water.

Gentle coaxing and a treat will help ease your Swissy into the down position.

to you to let him know that, while it may not be fun, the reward of your approval is worth his effort.

Start with the puppy on your left side in a sit position. Hold the leash right above his collar in your left hand. Have an extra-special treat, such as a small piece of cooked chicken or hot dog, in your right hand. Place it at the end of the pup's nose and steadily move your hand down and forward along the ground. Hold the leash to prevent a sudden

The verbal command "Stay" is reinforced with a hand signal.

have the dog sit on your left side. Hold the leash at waist level in your left hand and let the dog know that you have a treat in your closed right hand. Step forward on your right foot as you say "Stay." Immediately turn and stand directly in front of the dog, keeping your right hand up high so he'll keep his eye on the treat hand and maintain the sit position for a count of five. Return to your original position and offer the reward.

Increase the length of the sit/stay each time until the dog can hold it for at least 30 seconds without moving. After about a week of success, move out on your right foot and take two steps before turning to face the dog. Give the "Stay" hand signal (left palm back toward the dog's head) as you leave. He gets the treat when you return and he holds the sit/stay. Increase the distance that you walk away from him before turning until you reach the length of your training leash. But don't rush it! Go back to the beginning if he moves before he should. No matter what the lesson, never be upset by having to back up for a few days. The repetition and practice are what will make your dog reliable in these commands. It won't do any good to move on to something more difficult if the command is not mastered at the easier levels. Above all, even if you do get frustrated, never let your puppy know! Always keep a positive, upbeat attitude during training, which will transmit to your dog for positive results.

The down/stay is taught in the same way once the dog is completely reliable and steady with the down command. Again, don't rush it. With the dog in the down position on your left side,

TEACHER'S PET

Dogs are individuals, not robots, with many traits basic to their breed. Some, bred to work alone, are independent thinkers; others rely on you to call the shots. If you have enrolled in a training class, your instructor can offer alternative methods of training based on your individual dog's instincts and personality. You may benefit from using a different type of collar or switching to a class with different kinds of dogs.

step out on your right foot as you say "Stay." Return by walking around in back of the dog and into your original position. While you are training, it's okay to murmur something like "Hold on" to encourage him to stay put. When the dog will stay without moving when you are at a distance of 3–4 feet, begin to increase the length of time before you return. Be sure he holds the down on your return until you say "Okay." At that point, he gets his treat—just so he'll remember for next time that it's not over until it's over.

THE COME EXERCISE

No command is more important to the safety of your Swissy than "Come." It is what you should say every single time you see the puppy running toward you: "Benny, come! Good dog." During playtime, run a few feet away from the puppy and turn and tell him to "Come" as he is already running to you. You can go so far as to teach your puppy two things at once if you squat down and hold out your arms. As the pup gets close to you and you're saying "Good dog," bring your right arm in about waist high. Now he's also learning the hand signal, an excellent device should you be on the phone when you need to get him to come to you! You'll also both be one step ahead when you enter obedience classes.

COME AND GET IT!
The come command is your dog's safety signal. Until he is 99% perfect in responding, don't use the come command if you cannot enforce it. Practice on leash with treats or squeakers or whenever the dog is running to you. Never call him to come to you if he is to be corrected for a misdemeanor. Reward the dog with a treat and happy praise whenever he comes to you.

When the puppy responds to your well-timed "Come," try it with the puppy on the training leash. This time, catch him off guard, while he's sniffing a leaf or watching a bird: "Benny, come!" You may have to pause for a split second after his name to be sure you have his attention. If the puppy shows any sign of confusion, give the leash a mild jerk and take a couple of steps backward. Do not repeat the command. In this case, you should say "Good come" as he reaches you.

That's the number-one rule of training. Each command word is given just once. Anything more is nagging. You'll also notice that all commands are one word only. Even when they are actually two words, you say them as one.

Never call the dog to come to you—with or without his name—if you are angry or intend to correct him for some misbehavior. When correcting the pup, you go to him. Your dog must always connect "Come" with something pleasant and with your approval; then you can rely on his response.

Puppies, like children, have notoriously short attention spans, so don't overdo it with any of the training. Keep each lesson short. Break it up with a quick run around the yard or a ball toss, repeat the lesson and quit as soon as the pup gets it right. That way, you will always end with a "Good dog."

Life isn't perfect and neither are puppies. A time will come, often around ten months of age, when he'll become "selectively deaf" or choose to "forget" his name. He may respond by wagging his tail (and even seeming to smile at you) with a look that says "Make me!" Laugh, throw his favorite toy and skip the lesson you had planned. Pups will be pups!

THE HEEL EXERCISE

The second most important command to teach, after the come, is the heel. When you are walking your growing puppy, you need to be in control. Besides, it looks

> ### MORE PRAISE, LESS FOOD
>
> As you progress with your puppy's lessons, and the puppy is responding well, gradually begin to wean him off the treats by alternating the treats with times when you offer only verbal praise or a few pats on the dog's side. (Pats on the head are dominant actions, so he won't think they are meant to be praise.) Every lesson should end with the puppy's performing the correct action for that session's command. When he gets it right and you withhold the treat, the praise can be as long and lavish as you like. The commands are one word only, but your verbal praise can use as many words as you want—don't skimp!

terrible to be pulled and yanked down the street, and it's not much fun either. Your eight- to ten-week-old puppy will probably follow you everywhere, but that's his natural instinct, not your control over the situation. However, any time he does follow you, you can say "Heel" and be ahead of the game, as he will learn to associate this command with the action of following you before you even begin teaching him to heel.

There is a very precise, almost military, procedure for teaching your dog to heel. As with all other obedience training, begin with the dog on your left side. He will be in a very nice sit and you will have the training leash across your chest. Hold the loop and folded leash in your right hand. Pick up the slack leash above the dog in your left hand and hold it loosely at your side. Step out on your left foot as you say "Heel." If the puppy does not move, give a gentle tug or pat your left leg to get him started. If he surges ahead of you, stop and pull him back gently until he is at your side. Tell him to sit and begin again.

Walk a few steps and stop while the puppy is correctly beside you. Tell him to sit and give mild verbal praise. (More enthusiastic praise will encourage him to think the lesson is over.) Repeat the lesson, increasing the number of steps you take only as

long as the dog is heeling nicely beside you. When you end the lesson, have him hold the sit, then give him the "Okay" to let him know that this is the end of the lesson. Praise him so that he knows he did a good job.

The cure for excessive pulling (a common problem) is to stop when the dog is no more than 2 or 3 feet ahead of you. Guide him back into position and begin again. With a really determined puller, try switching to a head collar. When used properly, this will automatically turn the pup's head toward you so you can bring him back easily to the heel position. Give quiet, reassuring praise every time the leash goes slack and he's staying with you.

Staying and heeling can take a lot out of a dog, so provide playtime and free-running exercise to shake off the stress

With a dog as strong as the Swissy, teaching your dog to behave properly on lead is essential.

when the lessons are over. You don't want him to associate training with all work and no fun.

TAPERING OFF TIDBITS

Your dog has been watching you—and the hand that treats—throughout all of his lessons, and now it's time to break the treat habit. Begin by giving him treats at the end of each lesson only. Then start to give a treat after the end of only some of the lessons. At the end of every lesson, as well as during the lessons, be consistent with the praise. Your pup now doesn't know whether he'll get a treat or not, but he should keep performing well just in case! Finally, you will stop giving treat rewards entirely. Save them for something brand-new that you want to teach him. Keep up the praise and you'll always have a "good dog."

OBEDIENCE CLASSES

The advantages of an obedience class are that your dog will have to learn amid the distractions of other people and dogs and that your mistakes will be quickly corrected by the trainer. Teaching your dog along with a qualified instructor and other handlers who may have more dog experience than you is another plus of the class environment. The instructor and other handlers can help you to find the most efficient way of teaching your dog a command or exercise. It's often easier to learn by other people's mistakes than your own. You will also learn all of the requirements for competitive obedience trials, in which you can earn titles and go on to advanced jumping and retrieving exercises, which are fun for many dogs. Obedience classes build the foundation needed for many other canine activities (in which we humans are allowed to participate, too!).

TRAINING FOR OTHER ACTIVITIES

Once your dog has basic obedience under his collar and is 12 months of age, you can enter the world of agility training. Dogs think agility is pure fun, like being turned loose in an amusement park full of obstacles! In addition to agility, tracking tests are open to all "nosey" dogs (which would include all dogs!). For those who like to volunteer, there is the wonderful feeling of owning a therapy dog and visiting hospices, nursing homes and veterans' homes to bring smiles, comfort and companionship to those who live there.

Of course, in addition to all-breed events and activities, there are pursuits that are suited to the Swissy as a breed. Despite the fact that machinery now does a lot of work on modern farms, the Swissy still has a place as a working dog. The GSMD remains a cost-effective (not to mention cuddlier) alternative to machinery. The GSMD is an excellent means of transporting people and goods across a farm for relatively short distances; the breed is sometimes referred to as the "poor man's horse." The Swissy is a companion, a watchdog, a transporter of goods and people and a herding dog. It's easy to see why this breed is not easy to replace.

For people interested in using their pet Swissys as draft or working dogs, the same equipment is used on the farm as is used in competition. This equipment is available through draft or weight-pulling clubs. Once again, it is important that equipment fit appropriately and that the dog be in the very best of health. All training should be gradual and consistent.

Another common activity for the GSMD is to pull sleds or carts

built for people to ride in. This is especially fun for the children and the dog during the winter, as it allows the Swissy to combine his love of work and people.

Even if you don't have a farm on which your Swissy can work, he can be taught to do some simple chores around the house

that he will enjoy. You might teach him to carry a small basket of household items or to fetch the morning newspaper. The kids can teach the dog all kinds of tricks, from playing hide-and-seek to balancing a biscuit on his nose. A family dog is what rounds out the family. Everything he does, including sitting at your feet and gazing lovingly at you, represents the bonus of owning a dog.

You will be happy owning a properly trained, well-behaved pet, and your Swissy will be happy spending time with his beloved owner. Everyone's a winner!

PHYSICAL STRUCTURE OF THE GREATER SWISS MOUNTAIN DOG

Tail
Hock
Croup
Foot
Hip
Stifle
Thigh
Back
Flank
Withers
Brisket
Occiput
Neck
Foreleg
Pastern
Chest
Stop
Muzzle

GREATER SWISS MOUNTAIN DOG

BY LOWELL ACKERMAN DVM, DACVD

HEALTHCARE FOR A LIFETIME

When you own a dog, you become his healthcare advocate over his entire lifespan, as well as being the one to shoulder the financial burden of such care. Accordingly, it is worthwhile to focus on prevention rather than treatment, as you and your pet will both be happier.

Of course, the best place to have begun your program of preventive healthcare is with the initial purchase or adoption of your dog. There is no way of guaranteeing that your new furry friend is free of medical problems, but there are some things you can do to improve your odds. You certainly should have done adequate research into the Greater Swiss Mountain Dog and have selected your puppy carefully rather than buying on impulse. Health issues aside, a large number of pet abandonment and relinquishment cases arise from a mismatch between pet needs and owner expectations. This is entirely preventable with appropriate planning and finding a good breeder.

Regarding healthcare issues specifically, it is very difficult to make blanket statements about where to acquire a problem-free pet, but, again, a reputable breeder is your best bet. In an ideal situation you have the opportunity to see both parents, get references from other owners of the breeder's pups and see genetic-testing documentation for several generations of the litter's ancestors. At the very least, you must thoroughly investigate the Swissy and the problems inherent in the breed, as well as the genetic testing available to screen for hereditary problems. Genetic testing offers some important benefits, but is available for only a few disorders in a relatively small number of breeds and is not available for some of the most common genetic diseases, such as hip dysplasia, cataracts, epilepsy, cardiomyopathy, etc. This area of research is indeed exciting and increasingly important, and advances will continue to be made each year. In fact, recent research has shown that there is an equivalent dog gene for 75% of

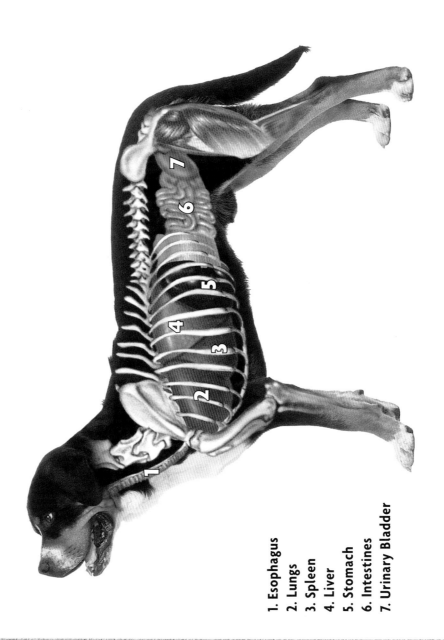

1. Esophagus
2. Lungs
3. Spleen
4. Liver
5. Stomach
6. Intestines
7. Urinary Bladder

INTERNAL ORGANS OF THE GREATER SWISS MOUNTAIN DOG

known human genes, so research done in either species is likely to benefit the other.

We've also discussed that evaluating the behavioral nature of your Swissy and that of his immediate family members is an important part of the selection process that cannot be overemphasized. It is sometimes difficult to evaluate temperament in puppies because certain behavioral tendencies, such as some forms of aggression, may not be immediately evident. More dogs are euthanized each year for behavioral reasons than for all medical conditions combined, so it is critical to take temperament issues seriously. Start with a well-balanced, friendly companion and put the time and effort into proper socialization, and you will both be rewarded with a valued relationship for the life of the dog.

Assuming that you have started off with a pup from healthy, sound stock, you then become responsible for helping your veterinarian keep your pet healthy. Some crucial things happen before you even bring your puppy home. Parasite control typically begins at two weeks of age, and vaccinations typically begin at six to eight weeks of age. A pre-pubertal evaluation is typically scheduled for about six months of age. At this time, a dental evaluation is done (since the adult teeth are

now in) and heartworm prevention is started. Neutering or spaying is most commonly done around six months of age

DENTAL WARNING SIGNS

A veterinary dental exam is necessary if you notice one or any combination of the following in your dog:

- Broken, loose or missing teeth
- Loss of appetite (which could be due to mouth pain or illness caused by infection)
- Gum abnormalities, including redness, swelling and bleeding
- Drooling, with or without blood
- Yellowing of the teeth or gumline, indicating tartar
- Bad breath

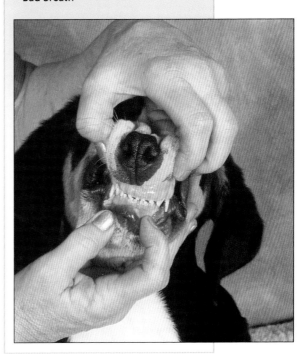

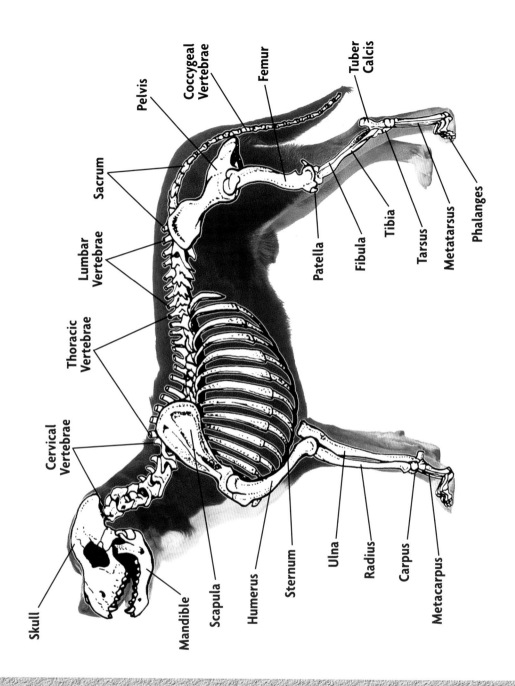

Coccygeal Vertebrae

Femur

Tuber Calcis

Pelvis

Sacrum

Phalanges

Lumbar Vertebrae

Patella

Fibula

Tibia

Tarsus

Metatarsus

Thoracic Vertebrae

Cervical Vertebrae

Skull

Mandible

Scapula

Humerus

Sternum

Ulna

Radius

Carpus

Metacarpus

SKELETAL STRUCTURE OF THE GREATER SWISS MOUNTAIN DOG

although breeders often suggest that you wait to have a female Swissy spayed until after her first heat cycle, which may help in preventing her from developing urinary incontinence.

It is critical to commence regular dental care at home if you have not already done so. It may not sound very important, but most dogs have active periodontal disease by four years of age if they don't have their teeth cleaned regularly at home, not just at their veterinary exams. Dental problems lead to more than just bad "doggy breath." Gum disease can have very serious medical consequences. If you start brushing your dog's teeth and using antiseptic rinses from a young age, your dog will be accustomed to it and will not resist. The results will be healthy dentition, which your pet will need to enjoy a long, healthy life.

Although most dogs are considered adults at a year of age, larger breeds like the GSMD continue filling out up to about three or so years old. Even individual dogs within each breed have different healthcare requirements, so work with your veterinarian to determine what will be needed and what your role should be. This doctor-client relationship is important, because as vaccination guidelines change, there may not be an annual "vaccine visit" scheduled. You must make sure that you see your

TAKING YOUR DOG'S TEMPERATURE

It is important to know how to take your dog's temperature at times when you think he may be ill. It's not the most enjoyable task, but it can be done without too much difficulty. It's easier with a helper, preferably someone with whom the dog is friendly, so that one of you can hold the dog while the other inserts the thermometer.

Before inserting the thermometer, coat the end with petroleum jelly. Insert the thermometer slowly and gently into the dog's rectum about one inch. Wait for the reading, about two minutes. Be sure to remove the thermometer carefully and clean it thoroughly after each use.

A dog's normal body temperature is between 100.5 and 102.5 degrees F. Immediate veterinary attention is required if the dog's temperature is below 99 or above 104 degrees F.

veterinarian at least annually, even if no vaccines are due, because this is the best opportunity to coordinate healthcare activities and to make sure that no medical issues creep by unaddressed.

When your Swissy reaches three-quarters of his anticipated lifespan at around six or seven years of age, he is considered a "senior" and will require some special care. In general, if you've been taking great care of your canine companion throughout his formative and adult years, the transition to senior status should be a smooth one. Age is not a disease, and as long as everything is functioning as it should, there is no reason why most of late adulthood should not be rewarding for both you and your pet. This is especially true if you have tended to the details, such as regular veterinary visits, proper dental care, excellent nutrition and management of bone and joint issues.

At this stage in your Swissy's life, your veterinarian may want to schedule visits twice yearly, instead of once, to run some laboratory screenings, electrocardiograms and the like, and to change the diet to something more digestible. Catching problems early is the best way to manage them effectively. Treating the early stages of heart disease is so much easier than trying to intervene when there is more significant damage to the heart muscle. Similarly, managing the beginning of kidney problems is fairly routine if there is no significant kidney damage. Other problems, like cognitive dysfunction (similar to senility and Alzheimer's disease), cancer, diabetes and arthritis, are more common in older dogs, but all can be treated to help the dog live as many happy, comfortable years as possible. Just as in people, medical management is more effective (and less expensive) when you catch things early.

SELECTING A VETERINARIAN

There is probably no more important decision that you will make regarding your pet's health-care than the selection of his doctor. A good vet for the Swissy is one who is familiar with breed-specific health issues and the care of large-breed dogs. Your pet's veterinarian will be a pediatrician, family-practice physician and gerontologist, depending on the dog's life stage, and will be the individual who makes recommendations regarding issues such as when specialists need to be consulted, when diagnostic testing and/or therapeutic intervention is needed and when you will need to seek outside emergency and critical-care services. Your vet will act as your advocate and liaison throughout these processes.

Everyone has his own idea about what to look for in a vet, an individual who will play a big role in his dog's (and, of course, his own) life for many years to come. For some, it is the compassionate caregiver with whom they hope to develop a professional relationship to span the lives of their dogs and even their future pets. For others, they are seeking a clinician with keen diagnostic and therapeutic insight who can deliver state-of-the-art healthcare. Still others need a veterinary facility that is open evenings and weekends, is in close proximity or provides mobile veterinary services to accommodate their schedules; these people may not much mind that their dogs might see different veterinarians on each visit. Just as we have different reasons for selecting our own healthcare professionals (e.g., covered by insurance plan, expert in field, convenient location, etc.), we should not expect that there is a one-size-fits-all recommendation for selecting a veterinarian and veterinary practice. The best advice is to be honest in your assessment of what you expect from a veterinary practice and to conscientiously research the options in your area. You will quickly appreciate that not all veterinary practices are the same, and you will be happiest with one that truly meets your needs.

There is another point to be considered in the selection of veterinary services. Not that long ago, a single veterinarian would attempt to manage all medical and surgical issues as they arose. That was often problematic, because veterinarians are trained in many species and many diseases, and it was just impossible for general veterinary practitioners to be experts in every species, every breed, every field and every ailment. However, just as in the human healthcare fields, specialization has allowed general practitioners to concentrate on primary healthcare delivery, especially

Most puppies get their first shots from the breeder, and your vet will continue the vaccination schedule.

wellness and the prevention of infectious diseases, and to utilize a network of specialists to assist in the management of conditions that require specific expertise and experience. Thus there are now many types of veterinary specialists, including dermatologists, cardiologists, ophthalmologists, surgeons, internists, oncologists, neurologists, behaviorists, criticalists and others to help primary-care veterinarians deal with complicated medical challenges. In most cases, specialists see cases referred by primary-care veterinarians, make diagnoses and set up management plans. From there, the animals' ongoing care is

COMMON INFECTIOUS DISEASES

Let's discuss some of the diseases that create the need for vaccination in the first place. Following are the major canine infectious diseases and a simple explanation of each.

Rabies: A devastating viral disease that can be fatal in dogs and people. In fact, vaccination of dogs and cats is an important public-health measure to create a resistant animal buffer population to protect people from contracting the disease. Vaccination schedules are determined on a government level and are not optional for pet owners; rabies vaccination is required by law in all 50 states.

Parvovirus: A severe, potentially life-threatening disease that is easily transmitted between dogs. There are four strains of the virus, but it is believed that there is significant "cross-protection" between strains that may be included in individual vaccines.

Distemper: A potentially severe and life-threatening disease with a relatively high risk of exposure, especially in certain regions. In very high-risk distemper environments, young pups may be vaccinated with human measles vaccine, a related virus that offers cross-protection when administered at four to ten weeks of age.

Hepatitis: Caused by canine adenovirus type 1 (CAV-1), but since vaccination with the causative virus has a higher rate of adverse effects, cross-protection is derived from the use of adenovirus type 2 (CAV-2), a cause of respiratory disease and one of the potential causes of canine cough. Vaccination with CAV-2 provides long-term immunity against hepatitis, but relatively less protection against respiratory infection.

Canine cough: Also called tracheobronchitis, actually a fairly complicated result of viral and bacterial offenders; therefore, even with vaccination, protection is incomplete. Wherever dogs congregate, canine cough will likely be spread among them. Intranasal vaccination with *Bordetella* and parainfluenza is the best safeguard, but the duration of immunity does not appear to be very long, typically a year at most. These are non-core vaccines, but vaccination is sometimes mandated by boarding kennels, obedience classes, dog shows and other places where dogs congregate to try to minimize spread of infection.

Leptospirosis: A potentially fatal disease that is more common in some geographic regions. It is capable of being spread to humans. The disease varies with the individual "serovar," or strain, of *Leptospira* involved. Since there does not appear to be much cross-protection between serovars, protection is only as good as the likelihood that the serovar in the vaccine is the same as the one in the pet's local environment. Problems with *Leptospira* vaccines are that protection does not last very long, side effects are not uncommon and a large percentage of dogs (perhaps 30%) may not respond to vaccination.

Borrelia burgdorferi: The cause of Lyme disease, the risk of which varies with the geographic area in which the pet lives and travels. Lyme disease is spread by deer ticks in the eastern US and western black-legged ticks in the western part of the country, and the risk of exposure is high in some regions. Lameness, fever and inappetence are most commonly seen in affected dogs. The extent of protection from the vaccine has not been conclusively demonstrated.

Coronavirus: This disease has a high risk of exposure, especially in areas where dogs congregate, but it typically causes only mild to moderate digestive upset (diarrhea, vomiting, etc.). Vaccines are available, but the duration of protection is believed to be relatively short and the effectiveness of the vaccine in preventing infection is considered low.

There are many other vaccinations available, including those for *Giardia* and canine adenovirus-1. While there may be some specific indications for their use, and local risk factors to be considered, they are not widely recommended for most dogs.

returned to their primary-care veterinarians. This important team approach to your pet's medical-care needs has provided opportunities for advanced care and an unparalleled level of quality to be delivered.

With all of the opportunities for your Greater Swiss Mountain Dog to receive high-quality veterinary medical care, there is another topic that needs to be addressed at the same time—cost. It's been said that you can have excellent healthcare or inexpensive healthcare, but never both; this is as true in veterinary medicine as it is in human medicine. While veterinary costs are a fraction of what the same services cost in the human healthcare arena, it is still difficult to deal with unanticipated medical costs, especially since they can easily creep into hundreds or even thousands of dollars if specialists or emergency services become involved. However, there are ways of managing these risks. The easiest is to buy pet health insurance and realize that its foremost purpose is not to cover routine healthcare visits but rather to serve as an umbrella for those rainy days when your pet needs medical care and you don't want to worry about whether or not you can afford that care.

Pet insurance policies are very cost-effective (and very inexpensive by human health-insurance standards), but make sure that you buy the policy long before you intend to use it (preferably starting in puppyhood, because coverage will exclude pre-existing conditions) and that you are actually buying an indemnity insurance plan from an insurance company that is regulated by your state or province. Many insurance policy look-alikes are actually discount clubs that are redeemable only at specific locations and for specific services. An indemnity plan covers your pet at almost all veterinary, specialty and emergency practices and is an excellent way to manage your pet's ongoing healthcare needs.

VACCINATIONS AND INFECTIOUS DISEASES

There has never been an easier time to prevent a variety of infectious diseases in your dog, but the advances we've made in veterinary medicine come with a price—choice. Now while it may seem that choice regarding your pet's vaccinations is a good thing (and it is), it also has never been more difficult for the pet owner (or the veterinarian) to make an informed decision about the best way to protect pets through vaccination.

Years ago, it was just accepted that puppies got a starter series of vaccinations and then annual "boosters" throughout their lives to keep them protected. As more and more vaccines became available, consumers wanted the convenience of having all of that protection in a single injection. The result was "multivalent" vaccines that crammed a lot of protection into a single syringe. The manufacturers' recommendations were to give the vaccines annually, and this was a simple enough protocol to follow. However, as veterinary medicine has become more sophisticated and we have started looking more at healthcare quandaries rather than convenience, it became necessary to reevaluate the situation and deal with some tough questions. It is important to realize that whether or not to use a particular vaccine depends on the risk of contracting the disease against which it protects, the severity of the disease if it is contracted, the duration of immunity provided by the vaccine, the safety of the product and the needs of the individual animal. In a very general sense, rabies, distemper, hepatitis and parvovirus are considered core vaccine needs, while parainfluenza, *Bordetella bronchiseptica*, leptospirosis, coronavirus and borreliosis (Lyme disease) are considered non-core needs and best reserved for animals that demonstrate reasonable risk of contracting the diseases.

NEUTERING/SPAYING

Sterilization procedures (neutering for males/spaying for females) are meant to accomplish several purposes. While the underlying premise is to address the risk of pet overpopulation, there are some medical and behavioral benefits to the surgeries as well. For females, spaying prior to the first estrus (heat cycle) leads to a marked reduction in the risk of mammary cancer and other serious female health problems. Owners of female GSMDs must discuss spaying with their breeders and vets. Some feel that spaying after the first but before the second heat cycle will reduce the risk of the dog's developing urinary incontinence while still preserving some of the health benefits of spaying before the first estrus. Aside from health benefits, spaying also means no manifestations of "heat" to attract male dogs and no bleeding in the house. For males, there is prevention of testicular cancer and a reduction in the risk of prostate problems. In both sexes there may be some limited reduction in aggressive behaviors toward other dogs and some diminishing of urine marking, roaming and mounting.

While neutering and spaying do indeed prevent animals from contributing to pet overpopulation, even no-cost and low-cost neutering options have not eliminated the problem. Perhaps one of the main reasons for this is that individuals that intentionally breed their dogs and those that allow their animals to run at large are the main causes of unwanted offspring. Also, animals in shelters are often there because they were abandoned or relinquished, not because they came from unplanned matings. Neutering/spaying is important, but it should be considered in the context of the real causes of animals' ending up in shelters and eventually being euthanized.

One of the important consid-erations regarding neutering is that it is a surgical procedure. This sometimes gets lost in discussions of low-cost procedures and commoditization of the process. In females, spaying is specifically referred to as an ovariohysterectomy. In this procedure, a midline incision is made in the abdomen and the entire uterus and both ovaries are surgically removed. While this is a major invasive surgical procedure, it usually has few complications, because it is typically performed on healthy young animals. However, it is major surgery, as any woman who has had a hysterectomy will attest.

In males, neutering has traditionally referred to castration, which involves the surgical removal of both testicles. While

still a significant piece of surgery, there is not the abdominal exposure that is required in the female surgery. In addition, there is now a chemical sterilization option, in which a solution is injected into each testicle, leading to atrophy of the sperm-producing cells. This can typically be done under sedation rather than full anesthesia. This is a relatively new approach, and there are no long-term clinical studies yet available.

Neutering/spaying is typically done around six months of age at most veterinary hospitals, although techniques have been pioneered to perform the procedures in animals as young as eight weeks of age. In general, the surgeries on the very young animals are done for the specific reason of sterilizing them before they go to their new homes. This is done in some shelter hospitals for assurance that the animals will definitely not produce any pups. Otherwise, these organizations need to rely on owners to comply with their wishes to have the animals "altered" at a later date, something that does not always happen.

There are some exciting immunocontraceptive "vaccines" currently under development, and there may be a time when contra-ception in pets will not require surgical procedures. We anxiously await these developments.

A scanning electron micrograph of a dog flea, *Ctenocephalides canis*, on dog hair.

EXTERNAL PARASITES

FLEAS

Fleas have been around for millions of years and, while we have better tools now for controlling them than at any time in the past, there still is little chance that they will end up on an endangered species list. Actually, they are very well adapted to living on our pets, and they continue to adapt as we make advances.

The female flea can consume 15 times her weight in blood during active reproduction and can lay as many as 40 eggs a day. These eggs are very resistant to the effects of insecticides. They hatch into larvae, which then mature and spin cocoons. The immature fleas reside in this pupal stage until the time is right for feeding. This pupal stage is also very resistant to the effects of insecticides, and pupae can last in the environment without feeding for many months. Newly emergent fleas are attracted to animals by the warmth of the animals' bodies, movement and exhaled carbon dioxide. However, when they first emerge from their cocoons, they orient towards light; thus when an animal passes between a flea and the light source, casting a shadow, the flea pounces and starts to feed. If the animal turns out to be a dog or cat, the reproductive cycle continues. If the flea lands on another type of animal, including a person, the flea will bite but will then look for a more appropriate host. An emerging adult flea can survive without feeding for up to 12 months but, once it tastes blood, it can survive off its host for only 3 to 4 days.

It was once thought that fleas spend most of their lives in the environment, but we now know that fleas won't willingly jump off a dog unless leaping to another dog or when physically removed by brushing, bathing or other manipulation. Flea eggs, on the other hand, are shiny and smooth, and they roll off the animal and into the environment. The eggs, larvae and pupae then exist in the environment, but once the adult finds a susceptible animal, it's home sweet home until the flea is forced to seek refuge elsewhere.

Since adult fleas live on the animal and immature forms survive in the environment, a successful treatment plan must address all stages of the flea life cycle. There are now several safe and effective flea-control products that can be applied on a monthly

FLEA PREVENTION FOR YOUR DOG

- Discuss with your veterinarian the safest product to protect your dog, likely in the form of a monthly tablet or a liquid preparation placed on the back of the dog's neck.
- For dogs suffering from flea-bite dermatitis, a shampoo or topical insecticide treatment is required.
- Your lawn and property should be sprayed with an insecticide designed to kill fleas and ticks that lurk outdoors.
- Using a flea comb, check the dog's coat regularly for any signs of parasites.
- Practice good housekeeping. Vacuum floors, carpets and furniture regularly, especially in the areas that the dog frequents, and wash the dog's bedding weekly.
- Follow up house-cleaning with carpet shampoos and sprays to rid the house of fleas at all stages of development. Insect growth regulators are the safest option.

basis. These include fipronil, imidacloprid, selamectin and permethrin (found in several formulations). Most of these products have significant flea-killing rates within 24 hours. However, none of them will control the immature forms in the environment. To accomplish this, there are a variety of insect growth regulators that can be

THE FLEA'S LIFE CYCLE

What came first, the flea or the egg? This age-old mystery is more difficult to comprehend than the actual cycle of the flea. Fleas usually live only about four months. A female can lay 2,000 eggs in her lifetime.

Photo by Carolina Biological Supply Co.

Egg

After ten days of rolling around your carpet or under your furniture, the eggs hatch into larvae, which feed on various and sundry debris. In days or months, depending on the climate, the larvae spin cocoons and develop into the pupal or nymph stage, which quickly develop into fleas.

Larva

Photo by Carolina Biological Supply Co.

Pupa

These immature fleas must locate a host within 10 to 14 days or they will die. Only about 1% of the flea population exist as adult fleas, while the other 99% exist as eggs, larvae or pupae.

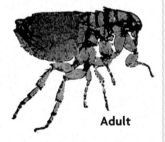

Adult

KILL FLEAS THE NATURAL WAY

If you choose not to go the route of conventional medication, there are some natural ways to ward off fleas:

- Dust your dog with a natural flea powder, composed of such herbal goodies as rosemary, wormwood, pennyroyal, citronella, rue, tobacco powder and eucalyptus.
- Apply diatomaceous earth, the fossilized remains of single-cell algae, to your carpets, furniture and pet's bedding. Even though it's not good for dogs, it's even worse for fleas, which will dry up swiftly and die.
- Brush your dog frequently, give him adequate exercise and let him fast occasionally. All of these activities strengthen the dog's immune system and make him more resistant to disease and parasites.
- Bathe your dog with a capful of pennyroyal or eucalyptus oil.
- Feed a natural diet, free of additives and preservatives. Add some fresh garlic and brewer's yeast to the dog's morning portion, as these items have flea-repelling properties.

sprayed into the environment (e.g., pyriproxyfen, methoprene, fenoxycarb) as well as insect development inhibitors such as lufenuron that can be administered. These compounds have no effect on adult fleas, but they stop immature forms from developing into adults. In years gone by, we relied heavily on toxic insecticides (such as organophosphates, organochlorines and carbamates) to manage the flea problem, but today's options are not only much safer to use on our pets but also safer for the environment.

TICKS

Ticks are members of the spider class (arachnids) and are blood-sucking parasites capable of transmitting a variety of diseases, including Lyme disease, ehrlichiosis, babesiosis and Rocky Mountain spotted fever. It's easy to see ticks on your own skin, but it is more of a challenge when your furry companion is affected. Whenever you happen to be planning a stroll in a tick-infested area (especially forests, grassy or wooded areas or parks) be prepared to do a thorough inspection of your dog afterward to search for ticks. Ticks can be tricky, so make sure you spend time looking in the ears, between the toes and everywhere else where a tick might hide. Ticks need to be attached for 24–72 hours before they transmit most of the diseases that they carry, so you do have a window of opportunity for some preventive intervention.

S.E.M. BY PHOTOTAKE.

A TICKING BOMB

There is nothing good about a tick's harpooning his nose into your dog's skin. Among the diseases caused by ticks are Rocky Mountain spotted fever, canine ehrlichiosis, canine babesiosis, canine hepatozoonosis and Lyme disease. If a dog is allergic to the saliva of a female wood tick, he can develop tick paralysis.

Female ticks live to eat and breed. They can lay between 4,000 and 5,000 eggs and they die soon after. Males, on the other hand, live only to mate with the females and continue the process as long as they are able. Most ticks live on multiple hosts before parasitizing dogs. The immature forms typically reside on grass and shrubs, waiting for susceptible animals to walk by. The larvae and nymph stages typically feed on wildlife.

If only a few ticks are present on a dog, they can be plucked out, but it is important to remove the entire head and mouthparts,

A scanning electron micrograph of the head of a female deer tick, *Ixodes dammini*, a parasitic tick that carries Lyme disease.

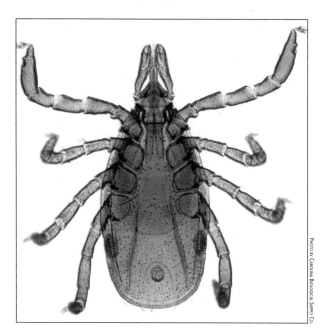

Photo by Carolina Biological Supply Co.

**Deer tick,
Ixodes dammini.**

disposed of in a container of alcohol or household bleach.

Some of the newer flea products, specifically those with fipronil, selamectin and permethrin, have effect against some, but not all, species of tick. Flea collars containing appropriate pesticides (e.g., propoxur, chlorfenvinphos) can aid in tick control. In most areas, such collars should be placed on animals in March, at the beginning of the tick season, and changed regularly. Leaving the collar on when the pesticide level is waning invites the development of resistance. Amitraz collars are also good for tick control, and the active ingredient does not interfere with other flea-control products. The ingredient helps prevent the attachment of ticks to the skin and will cause those ticks already on the skin to detach themselves.

which may be deeply embedded in the skin. This is best accomplished with forceps designed especially for this purpose; fingers can be used but should be protected with rubber gloves, plastic wrap or at least a paper towel. The tick should be grasped as closely as possible to the animal's skin and should be pulled upward with steady, even pressure. Do not squeeze, crush or puncture the body of the tick or you risk exposure to any disease carried by that tick. Once the ticks have been removed, the sites of attachment should be disinfected. Your hands should then be washed with soap and water to further minimize risk of contagion. The tick should be

TICK CONTROL
Removal of underbrush and leaf litter and the thinning of trees in areas where tick control is desired are recommended. These actions remove the cover and food sources for small animals that serve as hosts for ticks. With continued mowing of grasses in these areas, the probability of ticks' surviving is further reduced. A variety of insecticide ingredients (e.g., resmethrin, carbaryl, permethrin, chlorpyrifos, dioxathion and allethrin) are registered for tick control around the home.

MITES

Mites are tiny arachnid parasites that parasitize the skin of dogs. Skin diseases caused by mites are referred to as "mange," and there are many different forms seen in dogs. These forms are very different from one another, each one warranting an individual description.

Sarcoptic mange, or scabies, is one of the itchiest conditions that affects dogs. The microscopic *Sarcoptes* mites burrow into the superficial layers of the skin and can drive dogs crazy with itchiness. They are also communicable to people, although they can't complete their reproductive cycle on people. In addition to being tiny, the mites also are often difficult to find when trying to make a diagnosis. Skin scrapings from multiple areas are examined microscopically but, even then, sometimes the mites cannot be found.

Fortunately, scabies is relatively easy to treat, and there are a variety of products that will successfully kill the mites. Since the mites can't live in the environment for very long without feeding, a complete cure is usually possible within four to eight weeks.

Cheyletiellosis is caused by a relatively large mite, which sometimes can be seen even without a microscope. Often referred to as "walking dandruff," this also causes itching, but not usually as profound as with scabies.

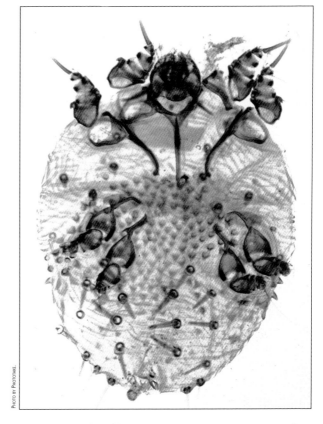

PHOTO BY PHOTOTAKE.

Sarcoptes scabiei, commonly known as the "itch mite."

While *Cheyletiella* mites can survive somewhat longer in the environment than scabies mites, they too are relatively easy to treat, being responsive to not only the medications used to treat scabies but also often to flea-control products.

Otodectes cynotis is the canine ear mite and is one of the more common causes of mange, especially in young dogs in shelters or pet stores. That's because the mites are typically present in large numbers and are quickly spread to

Micrograph of a dog louse, *Heterodoxus spiniger*. Female lice attach their eggs to the hairs of the dog. As the eggs hatch, the larval lice bite and feed on the blood. Lice can also feed on dead skin and hair. This feeding activity can cause hair loss and skin problems.

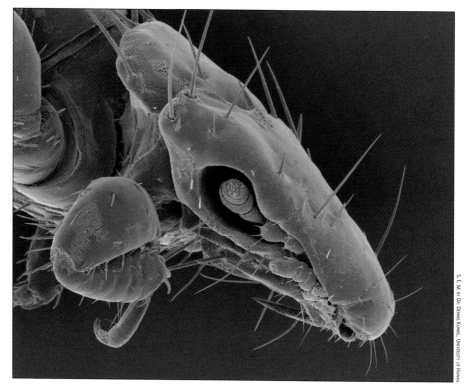

S. E. M. BY DR. DENNIS KUNKEL, UNIVERSITY OF HAWAII.

nearby animals. The mites rarely do much harm but can be difficult to eradicate if the treatment regimen is not comprehensive. While many try to treat the condition with ear drops only, this is the most common cause of treatment failure. Ear drops cause the mites to simply move out of the ears and as far away as possible (usually to the base of the tail) until the insecticide levels in the ears drop to an acceptable level—then it's back to business as usual! The successful treatment of ear mites requires treating all animals in the household with a systemic insecticide, such as selamectin, or a combination of miticidal ear drops combined with whole-body flea-control preparations.

Demodicosis, sometimes referred to as red mange, can be one of the most difficult forms of mange to treat. Part of the problem has to do with the fact that the mites live in the hair follicles and they are relatively well shielded from topical and systemic products. The main issue, however, is that demodectic mange typically results only when there is some underlying process interfering with the dog's immune system.

Since *Demodex* mites are

normal residents of the skin of mammals, including humans, there is usually a mite population explosion only when the immune system fails to keep the number of mites in check. In young animals, the immune deficit may be transient or may reflect an actual inherited immune problem. In older animals, demodicosis is usually seen only when there is another disease hampering the immune system, such as diabetes, cancer, thyroid problems or the use of immune-suppressing drugs. Accordingly, treatment involves not only trying to kill the mange mites but also discerning what is interfering with immune function and correcting it if possible.

Chiggers represent several different species of mite that don't parasitize dogs specifically, but do latch on to passersby and can cause irritation. The problem is most prevalent in wooded areas in the late summer and fall. Treatment is not difficult, as the mites do not complete their life cycle on dogs and are susceptible to a variety of miticidal products.

MOSQUITOES
Mosquitoes have long been known to transmit a variety of diseases to people, as well as just being biting pests during warm weather. They also pose a real risk to pets. Not only

ILLUSTRATION BY PHOTOTAKE

Illustration of *Demodex folliculoram.*

do they carry deadly heartworms but recently there also has been much concern over their involvement with West Nile virus. While we can avoid heartworm with the use of preventive medications, there are no such preventives for West Nile virus. The only method of prevention in endemic areas is active mosquito control. Fortunately, most dogs that have been exposed to the virus only developed flu-like symptoms and, to date, there have not been the large number of reported deaths in canines as seen in some other species.

MOSQUITO REPELLENT
Low concentrations of DEET (less than 10%), found in many human mosquito repellents, have been safely used in dogs but, in these concentrations, probably give only about two hours of protection. DEET may be safe in these small concentrations, but since it is not licensed for use on dogs, there is no research proving its safety for dogs. Products containing permethrin give the longest-lasting protection, perhaps two to four weeks. As DEET is not licensed for use on dogs, and both DEET and permethrin can be quite toxic to cats, appropriate care should be exercised. Other products, such as those containing oil of citronella, also have some mosquito-repellent activity, but typically have a relatively short duration of action.

S. E. M. BY DR. DENNIS KUNKEL, UNIVERSITY OF HAWAII; INSET BY TAM C. NGUYEN.

The ascarid roundworm *Toxocara canis,* showing the mouth with three lips. INSET: Photomicrograph of the roundworm *Ascaris lumbricoides.*

INTERNAL PARASITES: WORMS

ASCARIDS

Ascarids are intestinal roundworms that rarely cause severe disease in dogs. Nonetheless, they are of major public health significance because they can be transferred to people. Sadly, it is children who are most commonly affected by the parasite, probably from inadvertently ingesting ascarid-contaminated soil. In fact, many yards and children's sandboxes contain appreciable numbers of ascarid eggs. So, while ascarids don't bite dogs or latch onto their intestines to suck blood, they do cause some nasty medical conditions in children and are best eradicated from our furry friends. Because pups can start passing ascarid eggs by three weeks of age, most parasite-control programs begin at two weeks of age and are repeated every two weeks until pups are eight weeks old. It is important to

HOOKED ON ANCYLOSTOMA

Adult dogs can become infected by the bloodsucking nematodes we commonly call hookworms via ingesting larvae from the ground or via the larvae penetrating the dog's skin. It is not uncommon for infected dogs to show no symptoms of hookworm infestation. Sometimes symptoms occur within ten days of exposure. These symptoms can include bloody diarrhea, anemia, loss of weight and general weakness. Dogs pass the hookworm eggs in their stools, which serves as the vet's method of identifying the infestation. The hookworm larvae can encyst themselves in the dog's tissues and be released when the dog is experiencing stress.

Caused by an *Ancylostoma* species whose common host is the dog, cutaneous larval migrans affects humans, causing itching and lumps and streaks beneath the surface of the skin.

S. E. M. BY DR. DENNIS KUNKEL, UNIVERSITY OF HAWAII.

realize that bitches can pass ascarids to their pups even if they test negative prior to whelping. Accordingly, bitches are best treated at the same time as the pups.

HOOKWORMS

Unlike ascarids, hookworms do latch onto a dog's intestinal tract and can cause significant loss of blood and protein. Similar to ascarids, hookworms can be transmitted to humans, where they cause a condition known as cutaneous larval migrans. Dogs can become infected either by consuming the infective larvae or by the larvae's penetrating the skin directly. People most often get infected when they are lying on the ground (such as on a beach) and the larvae penetrate the skin. Yes, the larvae can penetrate through a beach blanket. Hookworms are typically susceptible to the same medications used to treat ascarids.

The hookworm *Ancylostoma caninum* infests the intestines of dogs. INSET: Note the row of teeth at the posterior end, used to anchor the worm to the intestinal wall.

WHIPWORMS

Whipworms latch onto the lower aspects of the dog's colon and can cause cramping and diarrhea. Eggs do not start to appear in the dog's feces until about three months after the dog was infected. This worm has a peculiar life cycle, which makes it more difficult to control than ascarids or hookworms. The good thing is that whipworms rarely are transferred to people.

Some of the medications used to treat ascarids and hookworms are also effective against whipworms, but, in general, a separate treatment protocol is needed. Since most of the medications are effective against the adults but not the eggs or larvae, treatment is typically repeated in three weeks, and then often in three

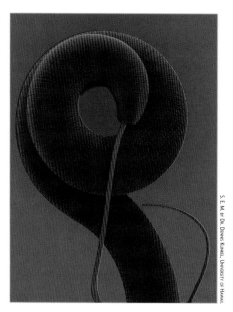

Adult whipworm, *Trichuris* sp., an intestinal parasite.

S. E. M. BY DR. DENNIS KUNKEL, UNIVERSITY OF HAWAII

WORM-CONTROL GUIDELINES

• Practice sanitary habits with your dog and home.
• Clean up after your dog and don't let him sniff or eat other dogs' droppings.
• Control insects and fleas in the dog's environment. Fleas, lice, cockroaches, beetles, mice and rats can act as hosts for various worms.
• Prevent dogs from eating uncooked meat, raw poultry and dead animals.
• Keep dogs and children from playing in sand and soil.
• Kennel dogs on cement or gravel; avoid dirt runs.
• Administer heartworm preventives regularly.
• Have your vet examine your dog's stool at your annual visits.
• Select a boarding kennel carefully so as to avoid contamination from other dogs or an unsanitary environment.
• Prevent dogs from roaming. Obey local leash laws.

months as well. Unfortunately, since dogs don't develop resistance to whipworms, it is difficult to prevent them from getting reinfected if they visit soil contaminated with whipworm eggs.

TAPEWORMS

There are many different species of tapeworm that affect dogs, but *Dipylidium caninum* is probably the most common and is spread by fleas. Flea larvae feed on organic debris and tapeworm eggs in the environment and, when a dog chews at himself and manages to ingest fleas, he might get a dose of tapeworm at the same time. The tapeworm then develops further in the intestine of the dog.

The tapeworm itself, which is a parasitic flatworm that latches onto the intestinal wall, is composed of numerous segments. When the segments break off into the intestine (as proglottids), they may accumulate around the rectum, like grains of rice. While this tapeworm is disgusting in its behavior, it is not directly communicable to humans (although humans can also get infected by swallowing fleas).

A much more dangerous tapeworm is *Echinococcus multilocularis*, which is typically found in foxes, coyotes and wolves. The eggs are passed in the feces and infect rodents, and, when dogs eat the rodents, the dogs can be infected by thousands of adult tapeworms. While the parasites don't cause many problems in dogs, this is considered the most lethal worm infection that people can get. Take appropriate precautions if you live in an area in which these tapeworms are found. Do not use mulch that may contain feces of dogs, cats or wildlife, and discourage your pets from hunting wildlife. Treat these tapeworm infections aggressively in pets, because if humans get infected, approximately half die.

HEARTWORMS

Heartworm disease is caused by the parasite *Dirofilaria immitis* and is seen in dogs around the world. A member of the roundworm group, it is spread between dogs by the bite of an infected mosquito. The mosquito injects infective larvae into the dog's skin with its bite, and these larvae develop under the skin for a period of time before making their way to the heart. There they develop into adults, which grow and create blockages of the heart, lungs and major blood vessels there. They also start producing offspring (microfilariae),

A dog tapeworm proglottid (body segment).

The dog tapeworm *Taenia pisiformis*.

S. E. M. BY DR. DENNIS KUNKEL, UNIVERSITY OF HAWAII.

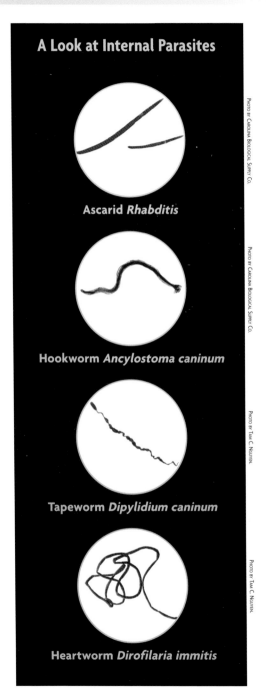

A Look at Internal Parasites

Ascarid *Rhabditis*

Hookworm *Ancylostoma caninum*

Tapeworm *Dipylidium caninum*

Heartworm *Dirofilaria immitis*

and these microfilariae circulate in the bloodstream, waiting to hitch a ride when the next mosquito bites. Once in the mosquito, the microfilariae develop into infective larvae and the entire process is repeated.

When dogs get infected with heartworm, over time they tend to develop symptoms associated with heart disease, such as coughing, exercise intolerance and potentially many other manifestations. Diagnosis is confirmed by either seeing the microfilariae themselves in blood samples or using immunologic tests (antigen testing) to identify the presence of adult heartworms. Since antigen tests measure the presence of adult heartworms and microfilarial tests measure offspring produced by adults, neither are positive until six to seven months after the initial infection. However, the beginning of damage can occur by fifth-stage larvae as early as three months after infection. Thus it is possible for dogs to be harboring problem-causing larvae for up to three months before either type of test would identify an infection.

The good news is that there are great protocols available for preventing heartworm in dogs. Testing is critical in the process, and it is important to understand the benefits as well as the limitations of such testing. All dogs six months of age or older that have not been on continuous heartworm-preventive medication should be

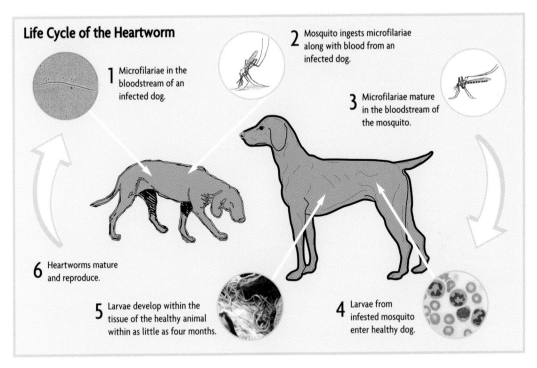

Life Cycle of the Heartworm

1 Microfilariae in the bloodstream of an infected dog.

2 Mosquito ingests microfilariae along with blood from an infected dog.

3 Microfilariae mature in the bloodstream of the mosquito.

4 Larvae from infested mosquito enter healthy dog.

5 Larvae develop within the tissue of the healthy animal within as little as four months.

6 Heartworms mature and reproduce.

screened with microfilarial or antigen tests. For dogs receiving preventive medication, periodic antigen testing helps assess the effectiveness of the preventives. The American Heartworm Society guidelines suggest that annual retesting may not be necessary when owners have absolutely provided continuous heartworm prevention. Retesting on a two- to three-year interval may be sufficient in these cases. However, your veterinarian will likely have specific guidelines under which heartworm preventives will be prescribed, and many prefer to err on the side of safety and retest annually.

It is indeed fortunate that heartworm is relatively easy to prevent, because treatments can be as life-threatening as the disease itself. Treatment requires a two-step process that kills the adult heartworms first and then the microfilariae. Prevention is obviously preferable; this involves a once-monthly oral or topical treatment. The most common oral preventives include ivermectin (not suitable for some breeds), moxidectin and milbemycin oxime; the once-a-month topical drug selamectin provides heartworm protection in addition to flea, some type of tick and other parasite controls.

THE ABCs OF
Emergency Care

Abrasions
Clean wound with running water or 3% hydrogen peroxide. Pat dry with gauze and spray with antibiotic. Do not cover.

Animal Bites
Clean area with soap and saline solution or water. Apply pressure to any bleeding area. Apply antibiotic ointment. Identify animal and contact the vet.

Antifreeze Poisoning
Induce vomiting and take dog to the vet.

Bee Sting
Remove stinger and apply soothing lotion or cold compress; give antihistamine in proper dosage.

Bleeding
Apply pressure directly to wound with gauze or towel for five to ten minutes. If wound does not stop bleeding, wrap wound with gauze and adhesive tape.

Bloat/Gastric Torsion
Immediately take the dog to the vet or emergency clinic; phone from car. No time to waste.

Burns
Chemical: Bathe dog with water and pet shampoo. Rinse in saline solution. Apply antibiotic ointment.

Acid: Rinse with water. Apply one part baking soda, two parts water to affected area.

Alkali: Rinse with water. Apply one part vinegar, four parts water to affected area.

Electrical: Apply antibiotic ointment. Seek veterinary assistance immediately.

Choking
If the dog is on the verge of collapsing, wedge a solid object, such as the handle of a screwdriver, between molars on one side of the mouth to keep mouth open. Pull tongue out. Use long-nosed pliers or fingers to remove foreign object. Do not push the object down the dog's throat. For small or medium dogs, hold dog upside down by hind legs and shake firmly to dislodge foreign object.

Chlorine Ingestion
With clean water, rinse the mouth and eyes. Give the dog water to drink; contact the vet.

Constipation
Feed dog 2 tablespoons bran flakes with each meal. Encourage drinking water. Mix $\frac{1}{4}$-teaspoon mineral oil in dog's food. Contact vet if persists.

Diarrhea
Withhold food for 12 to 24 hours. Feed dog anti-diarrheal with eyedropper. When feeding resumes, feed one part boiled hamburger, one part plain cooked rice, $\frac{1}{4}$- to $\frac{3}{4}$-cup four times daily. Contact vet if persists longer than 24 hours.

Dog Bite
Snip away hair around puncture wound; clean with 3% hydrogen peroxide; apply tincture of iodine. Identify biting dog and contact the vet. If wound appears deep, take the dog to the vet.

Frostbite
Wrap the dog in a heavy blanket. Warm affected area with a warm bath for ten minutes. Red color to skin will return with circulation; if tissues are pale after 20 minutes, contact the vet.

Use a portable, durable container large enough to contain all items.

Heat Stroke
Partially submerge the dog in cold water; if no response within ten minutes, contact the vet.

Hot Spots
Mix 2 packets Domeboro® with 2 cups water. Saturate cloth with mixture and apply to hot spots for 15 to 30 minutes. Apply antibiotic ointment. Repeat every six to eight hours.

Poisonous Plants
Wash affected area with soap and water. Cleanse with alcohol. For foxtail/grass, apply antibiotic ointment. Contact the vet if plant is ingested.

Rat Poison Ingestion
Induce vomiting. Keep dog calm, maintain dog's normal body temperature (use blanket or heating pad). Get to the vet for antidote.

Shock
Keep the dog calm and warm; call for veterinary assistance.

Snake Bite
If possible, bandage the area and apply pressure. If the area is not conducive to bandaging, use ice to control bleeding. Get immediate help from the vet.

Tick Removal
Apply flea and tick spray directly on tick. Wait one minute. Using tweezers or wearing plastic gloves, apply constant pull while grasping tick's body. Apply antibiotic ointment.

Vomiting
Restrict dog's water intake; offer a few ice cubes. Withhold food for next meal. Contact vet if vomiting persists longer than 24 hours.

DOG OWNER'S FIRST-AID KIT

- ❑ Gauze bandages/swabs
- ❑ Adhesive and non-adhesive bandages
- ❑ Antibiotic powder
- ❑ Antiseptic wash
- ❑ Hydrogen peroxide 3%
- ❑ Antibiotic ointment
- ❑ Lubricating jelly
- ❑ Rectal thermometer
- ❑ Nylon muzzle
- ❑ Scissors and forceps
- ❑ Eyedropper
- ❑ Syringe
- ❑ Anti-bacterial/fungal solution
- ❑ Saline solution
- ❑ Antihistamine
- ❑ Cotton balls
- ❑ Nail clippers
- ❑ Screwdriver/pen knife
- ❑ Flashlight
- ❑ Emergency phone numbers

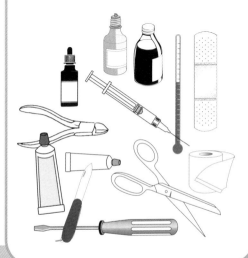

DON'T EAT THE DAISIES!

Many plants and flowers are beautiful to look at but can be highly toxic if ingested by your dog. Reactions range from abdominal pain and vomiting to convulsions and death. If the following plants are in your home, remove them. If they are outside your house or in your garden, avoid accidents by making sure your dog is never left unsupervised in those locations.

Azalea	Dumb cane	Mescal bean
Belladonna	Dutchman's breeches	Mushrooms
Bird of paradise	Elephant's ear	Nightshade
Bulbs	Hydrangea	Philodendron
Calla lily	Jack-in-the-pulpit	Poinsettia
Cardinal flower	Jasmine	*Prunus* species
Castor bean	Jimsonweed	Tobacco
Chinaberry tree	Larkspur	Yellow jasmine
Daphne	Laurel	Yews, *Taxus* species
	Lily of the valley	

THE EYES HAVE IT!

Eye disease is more prevalent among dogs than most people think, ranging from slight infections that are easily treated to serious complications that can lead to permanent sight loss. Eye diseases need veterinary attention in their early stages to prevent irreparable damage. This list provides descriptions of some common eye diseases:

Cataracts: Symptoms are white or gray discoloration of the eye lens and pupil, which causes fuzzy or completely obscured vision. Surgical treatment is required to remove the damaged lens and replace it with an artificial one.

Conjunctivitis: An inflammation of the mucous membrane that lines the eye socket, leaving the eyes red and puffy with excessive discharge. This condition is easily treated with antibiotics.

Corneal damage: The cornea is the transparent covering of the iris and pupil. Injuries are difficult to detect but manifest themselves in surface abnormality, redness, pain and discharge. Most infections of the cornea are treated with antibiotics and require immediate medical attention.

Dry eye: This condition is caused by deficient production of tears that lubricate and protect the eye surface. A telltale sign is yellow-green discharge. Left undiagnosed, your dog will experience considerable pain, infections and possibly blindness. Dry eye is commonly treated with antibiotics, although more advanced cases may require surgery.

Glaucoma: This is caused by excessive fluid pressure in the eye. Symptoms are red eyes, gray or blue discoloration, pain, enlarged eyeballs and loss of vision. Antibiotics sometimes help, but surgery may be needed.

Number-One Killer Disease in Dogs: CANCER

In every age, there is a word associated with a disease or plague that causes humans to shudder. In the 21st century, that word is "cancer." Just as cancer is the leading cause of death in humans, it claims nearly half the lives of dogs that die from a natural disease as well as half the dogs that die over the age of ten years.

Described as a genetic disease, cancer becomes a greater risk as the dog ages. Vets and dog owners have become increasingly aware of the threat of cancer to dogs. Statistics reveal that one dog in every five will develop cancer, the most common of which is skin cancer. Many cancers, including prostate, ovarian and breast cancer, can be avoided by spaying and neutering our dogs by the age of six months.

Early detection of cancer can save or extend a dog's life, so it is absolutely vital for owners to have their dogs examined by a qualified vet or oncologist immediately upon detection of any abnormality. Certain dietary guidelines have also proven to reduce the onset and spread of cancer. Foods based on fish rather than beef, due to the presence of Omega-3 fatty acids, are recommended. Other amino acids such as glutamine have significant benefits for canines, particularly those breeds that show a greater susceptibility to cancer.

Cancer management and treatments promise hope for future generations of canines. Since the disease is genetic, breeders should never breed a dog whose parents, grandparents and any related siblings have developed cancer. It is difficult to know whether to exclude an otherwise healthy dog from a breeding program, as the disease does not manifest itself until the dog's senior years.

RECOGNIZE CANCER WARNING SIGNS

Since early detection can possibly rescue your dog from becoming a cancer statistic, it is essential for owners to recognize the possible signs and seek the assistance of a qualified professional.

- Abnormal bumps or lumps that continue to grow
- Bleeding or discharge from any body cavity
- Persistent stiffness or lameness
- Recurrent sores or sores that do not heal
- Inappetence
- Breathing difficulties
- Weight loss
- Bad breath or odors
- General malaise and fatigue
- Eating and swallowing problems
- Difficulty urinating and defecating

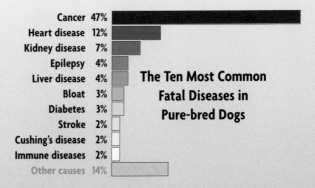

Cancer	47%
Heart disease	12%
Kidney disease	7%
Epilepsy	4%
Liver disease	4%
Bloat	3%
Diabetes	3%
Stroke	2%
Cushing's disease	2%
Immune diseases	2%
Other causes	14%

The Ten Most Common Fatal Diseases in Pure-bred Dogs

GREATER SWISS MOUNTAIN DOG

When we bring home a puppy, full of the energy and exuberance that accompanies youth, we hope for a long, happy and fulfilling relationship with the new family member. Even when we adopt an older dog, we look forward to the years of companionship ahead with a new canine friend. However, aging is inevitable for all creatures, and there will come a time when your Swissy reaches his senior years and will need special considerations and attention to his care.

WHEN IS MY DOG A "SENIOR"?
In general, pure-bred dogs are considered to have achieved senior status when they reach 75% of their breed's average lifespan, with lifespan being based on breed size along with breed-specific factors. Your GSMD has an average lifespan of eight to ten years and thus is considered a senior citizen at around six or seven years old.

Obviously, the old "seven dog years to one human year" theory is not exact. In puppyhood, a dog's year is actually comparable to more than seven human years, considering the puppy's rapid growth during his first year. Then, in adulthood, the ratio decreases. Regardless, the more viable rule of thumb is that the larger the dog, the shorter his expected lifespan. Of course, this can vary among individual dogs, with many living longer than expected, which we hope is the case! It is not uncommon to see Swissys in good health and with proper care reaching 12 or 13 years of age.

WHAT ARE THE SIGNS OF AGING?
By the time your dog has reached his senior years, you will know him very well, so the physical and behavioral changes that accompany aging should be noticeable to you. Humans and dogs share the most obvious physical sign of aging: gray hair. Graying often occurs first on the muzzle and face, around the eyes. Other telltale signs are the dog's overall decrease in activity. Your

older dog might be more content to nap and rest, and he may not show the same old enthusiasm when it's time to play in the yard or go for a walk. Other physical signs include significant weight loss or gain; more labored movement; skin and coat problems, possibly hair loss; sight and/or hearing problems; changes in toileting habits, perhaps seeming "unhouse-broken" at times; and tooth decay, bad breath or other mouth problems.

There are behavioral changes that go along with aging, too. There are numerous causes for behavioral changes. Sometimes a dog's apparent confusion results from a physical change like diminished sight or hearing. If his confusion causes him to be afraid, he may act aggressively or defensively. He may sleep more frequently because his daily walks, though shorter now, tire him out. He may begin to experience separation anxiety or, conversely, become less interested in petting and attention.

There also are clinical conditions that cause behavioral changes in older dogs. One such condition is known as canine cognitive dysfunction (familiarly known as "old-dog" syndrome). It can be frustrating for an owner whose dog is affected with cognitive dysfunction, as it can

result in behavioral changes of all types, most seemingly unexplain-able. Common changes include the dog's forgetting aspects of the daily routine, such as times to eat, go out for walks, relieve himself and the like. Along the same lines, you may take your dog out at the regular time for a potty trip and he may have no idea why he is there. Sometimes a placid dog will begin to show aggressive or possessive tenden-

> **WHAT A RELIEF!**
> Much like young puppies, older dogs do not have as much control over their excretory functions as they do as non-seniors. Their muscle control fades and, as such, they cannot "hold it" for as long as they used to. This is easily remedied by additional trips outside. If your dog's sight is failing, have the yard well lit at night and/or lead him to his relief site on lead. Incontinence should be discussed with your vet.

cies or, conversely, a hyperactive dog will start to "mellow out."

Disease also can be the cause of behavioral changes in senior dogs. Hormonal problems (Cushing's disease is common in older dogs), diabetes and thyroid disease can cause increased appetite, which can lead to aggression related to food guarding. It's better to be proactive with your senior dog, making more frequent trips to the vet if necessary and having bloodwork done to test for the diseases that can commonly befall older dogs.

This is not to say that, as dogs age, they all fall apart physically and become nasty in personality. The aforementioned changes are discussed to alert owners to the things that may happen as their dogs get older. Many hardy dogs remain active and alert well into old age. However, it can be frustrating and heartbreaking for owners to see their beloved dogs change physically and temperamentally. Just know that it's the same Swissy under there, and that he still loves you and appreciates your care, which he needs now more than ever.

HOW DO I CARE FOR MY AGING DOG?

Again, every dog is an individual in terms of aging. Your dog might reach the estimated "senior" age for Swissys and show no signs of slowing down. However, even if he shows no outward signs of aging, he should begin a senior-care program once he reaches the determined age. He may not show it, but he's not a pup anymore! By providing him with extra attention to his veterinary care at this age, you will be practicing good preventive medicine, ensuring that the rest of your dog's life will be as long, active, happy and healthy as possible. If you do notice indications of aging, such as graying and/or changes in sleeping, eating or toileting habits, this is a sign to set up a senior-care visit with your vet right away to make sure that these changes are not related to any health problems.

To start, senior dogs should visit the vet twice yearly for exams, routine tests and overall evaluations. Many veterinarians have special screening programs especially for senior dogs that can include a thorough physical exam; blood test to determine complete blood count; serum biochemistry test, which screens for liver, kidney and blood problems as well as cancer; urinalysis; and dental exams. With these tests, it can be determined whether your dog has any health problems; the results also establish a baseline for your pet against which future test results can be compared.

In addition to these tests, your vet may suggest additional testing, including an EKG, tests for glaucoma and other problems of the eye, chest x-rays, screening for tumors, blood pressure test, test for thyroid function and screening for parasites and reassessment of his preventive program. Your vet also will ask you questions about your dog's diet and activity level, what you

CAUSES OF CHANGE

Cognitive dysfunction may not be the cause of all changes in your older dog; illness and medication can also affect him. Things like diabetes, Cushing's disease, cancer and brain tumors are serious physical problems but can cause behavioral changes as well. Older dogs are more prone to these conditions, which should not be overlooked as possibilities for your dog's acting not like his "old self." Any significant changes in your senior's behavior are good reasons to take your dog to the vet for a thorough exam.

Your dog's reactions to medication can cause changes as well. The various types of corticosteroids are often cited as affecting a dog's behavior. If your vet prescribes any type of drug, discuss possible side effects before administering the medication to your dog.

feed and the amounts that you feed. This information, along with his evaluation of the dog's overall condition, will enable him to suggest proper dietary changes, if needed.

This may seem like quite a work-up for your pet, but veterinarians advise that older dogs need more frequent attention so that any health problems can be detected as early as possible. Serious conditions like kidney disease, heart disease and cancer may not present outward symptoms, or the problem may go undetected if the symptoms are mistaken by owners as just part of the aging process.

There are some conditions more common in elderly dogs that are difficult to ignore. Cognitive dysfunction shares much in common with senility and Alzheimer's disease, and dogs are not immune. Dogs can become confused and/or disoriented, lose their house-training, have abnormal sleep-wake cycles and interact differently with their owners. Be heartened by the fact that, in some ways, there are more treatment options for dogs with cognitive dysfunction than for people with similar conditions. There is good evidence that continued stimulation in the form of games, play, training and exercise can help to maintain cognitive function. There are also medications (such as seligiline) and antioxidant-fortified senior diets that have been shown to be beneficial.

Cancer is also a condition more common in the elderly. Although lung cancer, which is a major killer in humans, is relatively rare in dogs, almost all of the cancers seen in people are also seen in pets. If pets are getting regular physical examinations, cancers are often detected early. There are a variety of cancer therapies available today, and many pets continue to live happy lives with appropriate treatment.

Degenerative joint disease, often referred to as arthritis, is another malady common to both elderly dogs and humans. A lifetime of wear and tear on joints and running around at play eventually takes its toll and results in stiffness and difficulty in getting around. As dogs live longer and healthier lives, it is natural that they should eventually feel some of the effects of aging. Once again, if regular veterinary care has been available, your pet was not carrying extra pounds all those years and wearing those joints out before their time. If your pet was unfortunate enough to inherit hip dysplasia, osteochondritis dissecans or any of the other developmental orthopedic diseases, battling the onset of degenerative joint disease was probably a longstanding goal. In any case, there are now many effective remedies for managing degenerative joint disease and a number of remarkable surgeries as well.

Aside from the extra veterinary care, there is much you can do at home to keep your older dog in good condition. The dog's diet is an important factor. If your dog's appetite decreases, he will not be getting the nutrients he needs. He also will lose weight, which is unhealthy for a dog at a proper weight. Conversely, an older dog's metabolism is slower and he usually exercises less, but he should not be allowed to become obese. Obesity in an older dog is especially risky, because extra pounds mean extra stress on the body, increasing his vulnerability to heart disease. Additionally, the extra pounds make it harder for the dog to move about.

You should discuss age-related feeding changes with your vet. For a dog who has lost interest in food, it may be suggested to try some different types of food until you find something new that the dog likes. For an obese dog, a "light"-formula dog food or reducing food portions may be advised, along with exercise appropriate to his physical condition and energy level.

As for exercise, the senior dog should not be allowed to become a "couch potato" despite his old age. He may not be able to handle the old routine of long walks and vigorous games of fetch, but he still needs to get up and get moving. Keep up with your daily walks, but keep the distances shorter and let your dog set the pace. If he gets to the point where he's not up for walks, let him stroll around the yard. On the other hand, many dogs remain very active in their

CANINE COGNITIVE DYSFUNCTION

"OLD-DOG" SYNDROME

There are many ways for you to evaluate old-dog syndrome. Veterinarians have defined canine cognitive dysfunction as the gradual deterioration of cognitive abilities, indicated by changes in the dog's behavior. When a dog changes his routine response, and maladies have been eliminated as the cause of these behavioral changes, then canine cognitive dysfunction is the usual diagnosis.

More than half the dogs over eight years old suffer from some form of this syndrome. The older the dog, the more chance he has of suffering from it. In humans, doctors often dismiss the canine cognitive dysfunction behavioral changes as part of "winding down."

There are four major signs of canine cognitive dysfunction: frequent potty accidents inside the home, sleeping much more or much less than normal, acting confused and failing to respond to social stimuli.

SYMPTOMS

FREQUENT POTTY ACCIDENTS
• Urinates in the house.
• Defecates in the house.
• Doesn't signal that he wants to go out.

FAILURE TO RESPOND TO SOCIAL STIMULI
• Comes to people less frequently, whether called or not.
• Doesn't tolerate petting for more than a short time.
• Doesn't come to the door when you return home.

CONFUSION
• Goes outside and just stands there.
• Appears confused with a faraway look in his eyes.
• Hides more often.
• Doesn't recognize friends.
• Doesn't come when called.
• Walks around listlessly and without a destination.

SLEEP PATTERNS
• Awakens more slowly.
• Sleeps more than normal during the day.
• Sleeps less during the night.

senior years, so base changes to the exercise program on your own individual dog and what he's capable of. Don't worry, your Swissy will let you know when it's time to rest.

Keep up with your grooming routine as you always have. Be extra diligent about checking the skin and coat for problems. Older dogs can experience thinning coats as a normal aging process, but they can also lose hair as a result of medical problems. Some thinning is normal, but patches of baldness or the loss of significant amounts of hair is not.

Hopefully, you've been regular with brushing your dog's teeth throughout his life. Healthy teeth directly affect overall good health. We already know that bacteria from gum infections can enter the dog's body through the damaged gums and travel to the organs. At a stage in life when his organs don't function as well as they used to, you don't want anything to put additional strain on them. Clean teeth also contribute to a healthy immune system. Offering the dental-type chews in addition to toothbrushing can help, as they remove plaque and tartar as the dog chews.

Along with the same good care you've given him all of his life, pay a little extra attention to your dog in his senior years and keep up with twice-yearly trips to the vet. The sooner a problem is uncovered, the greater the chances of a full recovery.

SAYING GOODBYE

While you can help your dog live as long a life as possible, you can't help him live forever. A dog's lifespan is short when compared to that of a human, so it is inevitable that pet owners will experience loss. To many, losing a beloved dog is like losing a family member. Our dogs are part of our lives every day; they

> ### RUBDOWN REMEDY
> A good remedy for an aching dog is to give him a gentle massage each day, or even a few times a day if possible. This can be especially beneficial before your dog gets out of his bed in the morning. Just as in humans, massage can decrease pain in dogs, whether the dog is arthritic or just afflicted by the stiffness that accompanies old age. Gently massage his joints and limbs, as well as petting him on his entire body. This can help his circulation and flexibility and ease any joint or muscle aches. Massaging your dog has benefits for you, too; in fact, just petting our dogs can cause reduced levels of stress and lower our blood pressure. Massage and petting also help you find any previously undetected lumps, bumps or other abnormalities. Often these are not visible and only turn up by being felt.

are our true loyal friends and always seem to know when it's time to comfort us, to celebrate with us or to just provide the company of a caring friend. Even when we know that our dog is nearing his final days, we can never quite prepare for his being gone.

Many dogs live out long lives and simply die of old age. Others unfortunately are taken suddenly by illness or accident, and still others find their senior years compromised by disease and physical problems. In some of these cases, owners find themselves having to make difficult decisions.

EUTHANASIA

When the end comes for a beloved pet, it is a very difficult time for the owners. This time is made even more difficult when the owners are faced with making a choice regarding euthanasia, more commonly known as having a very sick or very aged dog "put to sleep" or "put down."

Veterinary euthanasia can be defined as the act of ending the life of a pet suffering from a terminal illness or an incurable condition. The usual procedure is that the animal is injected with a concentrated dose of anesthesia, causing unconsciousness within a few seconds and death soon after. This process is painless for the dog; the only discomfort he may feel is the prick of the needle, the same as he would with any other injection.

The decision of whether or not to euthanize is undoubtedly the hardest that owners have to make regarding their pets. It is a very emotional decision, yet it requires much clear thinking, discussion with the vet and, of course, discussion with all family members. During this time, owners will experience many different feelings: guilt, sadness, possibly anger at having to make this type of decision. Many times, it is hard to actually come to a decision, thinking that maybe the dog will miraculously recover or that maybe he will succumb to his illness, making the decision no longer necessary.

When faced with the decision to euthanize, you must take many things into consideration; first and foremost, what is best for your dog? Hopefully you have a good relationship with a vet whose medical opinion you trust and with whom you can discuss your decision openly and honestly. Remember that good vets are animal lovers, too, and want the best for their patients. Your vet should talk to you about your dog's condition and the reality of what the rest of his days will be like; will he be able to live out his days relatively comfortably or will the rest of his life be filled with pain? Many feel that euthanasia is the way to mercifully end a pet's suffering.

You have many factors to consider. Of course, you will speak with your vet and will involve all members of the family in each step of the decision-making process. Some of the things to think about include the current quality of your pet's life, whether he is constantly ill and/or in pain, whether there are things you can do to give him a comfortable life even if he has an incurable condition, whether you've explored all treatment problems, whether you've discussed the behavioral aspects of your pet's problems with an expert and whether you've thoroughly discussed with the vet your dog's prognosis and the likelihood of his ever again enjoying a normal life.

Of course, the aforementioned considerations present just some of the things that you will need to think about. You will have many questions and concerns of your own. Never feel pressured; take time to make a decision with which you will be comfortable.

If you've come to the decision that euthanasia is the right choice for your pet, there are a few further, equally heartrending, choices to make. Do you or another family member want to be present with your dog during the procedure? How will you say goodbye? Should you arrange for someone to accompany you to the vet for support so that you don't have to drive in a state of grief? Again, your emotions will be running high during this very difficult time, so think your decisions through clearly and rely on the support of family and friends.

THE GRIEVING PROCESS

Our pets are such big parts of our lives that, of course, we grieve for them when they pass away. To some, the loss of a pet affects them just as the loss of a friend or family member would. To many, dogs are true friends and family members.

Grieving over your pet is normal; in fact, it is necessary. The grieving process is the same, whether for a human or a pet. During this time you may want to seek the support of other animal lovers who have experienced the same thing, as they are sure to understand your feelings, offer a sympathetic ear and offer kind advice. Those without pets may not grasp the true scope of what you are going through, but hopefully they will still acknowledge your pain and offer condolences. Your response to your pet's death and your mourning are very personal, and you do not have to justify your feelings to anyone. Those who do not appreciate the value of a beloved pet obviously have not been blessed with the fulfillment that a pet's companionship brings.

That being said, there are many people who will completely understand your grief. They include people who knew your pet well, like friends, your vet or your groomer, as well as other pet lovers, maybe in a support group or pet-bereavement website. There are many places online where pet lovers gather to share their grief as well as their cherished memories. You likely also will be able to find bereavement counselors or discussion groups that meet in your area. You will also find comfort in your religious beliefs and can seek the support of clergy members.

Despite your sadness, you can find happiness in the time that you and your pet spent together. Your memories will always remind you of how your life was enriched by your Swissy.

WHAT'S NEXT?

Of course, following the death of a beloved pet, each person goes through a period of mourning. As time goes on and an owner becomes more accepting of the fact that his pet has passed on, his thoughts may turn to how to fill the void that his cherished companion has left behind. For some, dealing with and accept-

Many cities have pet cemeteries conveniently located. Your vet can assist you in locating one.

ance of a pet's death takes longer than others. Everyone grieves differently, so each person should take the time that he or she needs to start feeling better. A source of comfort for many, when they are ready, is to add a new pet to the home, while others feel as if they are betraying their departed friend by doing so. As time passes, you will decide how best to move on, so don't feel the need to rush into anything before you are absolutely ready. Allow yourself the time that you need to mourn and to heal.

If you decide that you'd like to add a new pet to the household, don't feel guilty. You are not trying to "replace" your dog, nor should you, but giving a new puppy or adult dog a new home is the most sincere way of honoring the memory of your beloved pet. No dog will ever replace another, but a new dog will create new happiness and new memories. Do you want a new puppy? Chances are, if your aging dog had battled with illness, you had put much time and effort into his care. Puppies require just as much time and effort; are you ready to start over? Many owners enjoy the aspect of raising a dog from youth and the special dog/owner bond that results. If you stayed in contact with your dog's breeder throughout the dog's life, you have a good place to begin your puppy search.

Another wonderful option is to look into adopting an adult dog from a rescue program or shelter. There are many wonderful dogs out there who end up homeless because of bad decision-making on the part of their former owners. Thinking of the special relationship that you shared with your dog, maybe you'd like to give one of these deserving dogs a second chance?

If you'd like another Greater Swiss Mountain Dog, start by contacting the Greater Swiss Mountain Dog Club of America, which can refer you to the rescue contact closest to you. You may decide on another breed to avoid comparison with your departed friend, or you may decide to take a trip to your local animal shelter to see whether you hit it off with one of the dogs there.

When selecting an adult dog, you must find out as much about the dog's past as possible so that you understand his temperament and how best to help him fit into your home. Some dogs may have special problems that can be overcome with the help of a dedicated owner, but many are just normal dogs who ended up in unfortunate circumstances and are now just looking for families to love and who will love them.

If you are not ready for a new dog, there are other ways that you can enjoy canine companionship. Perhaps you'd like to become involved at your local shelter or with breed rescue. That way, you can still spend time with dogs, and it will be fulfilling for you to know that you are helping them. You may even decide to provide a foster home for adoptable dogs.

However you decide to deal with your grief, keep your memories close to you. Your dog may no longer be with you, but you will always have the happiness of your wonderful years together. Hopefully those memories will make you a dog lover for life!

SHOWING YOUR

GREATER SWISS MOUNTAIN DOG

Is dog showing in your blood? Are you excited by the idea of gaiting your handsome Greater Swiss Mountain Dog around the ring to the thunderous applause of an enthusiastic audience? Are you certain that your beloved Swissy is flawless? You are not alone! Every loving owner thinks that his dog has no faults, or too few to mention. No matter how many times an owner reads the breed standard, he cannot find any faults in his aristocratic companion dog. If this sounds like you, and if you are considering entering your GSMD in a dog show, here are some basic questions to ask yourself:

- Did you purchase a "show-quality" puppy from the breeder?
- Is your puppy at least six months of age?
- Does the puppy exhibit correct show type for his breed?
- Does your puppy have any disqualifying faults?
- Is your GSMD registered with the American Kennel Club?
- How much time do you have to devote to training, grooming, conditioning and exhibiting your dog?
- Do you understand the rules and regulations of a dog show?
- Do you have time to learn how to show your dog properly?
- Do you have the financial resources to invest in showing your dog?
- Will you show the dog yourself or hire a professional handler?
- Do you have a vehicle that can

Gaiting a Swissy in the show ring to demonstrate his powerful movement requires practice and skill.

began as a novice and worked his way up to the Group ring. It's the "working your way up" part that you must keep in mind.

Assuming that you have purchased a puppy of the correct type and quality for showing, let's begin to examine the world of showing and what's required to get started. Although the entry fee into a dog show is nominal, there are lots of other hidden costs involved with "finishing" your Swissy, that is, making him a champion. Things like equipment, travel, training and conditioning all cost money. A more serious campaign will include fees for a professional handler, boarding, cross-country travel and advertising. Top-winning show dogs can represent a very considerable investment—over $100,000 has been spent in campaigning some dogs. (The investment can be less, of course, for owners who don't use professional handlers.)

Many owners, on the other hand, enter their "average" Swissys in dog shows for the fun and enjoyment of it. Dog showing makes an absorbing hobby, with many rewards for dogs and owners alike. If you're having fun, meeting other people who share your interests and enjoying the overall experience, you likely will catch the "bug." Once the dog-show bug bites, its effects can last a

accommodate your weekend trips to the dog shows?

Success in the show ring requires more than a pretty face, a wagging tail and a pocketful of liver. Even though dog shows can be exciting and enjoyable, the sport of conformation makes great demands on the exhibitors and the dogs. Winning exhibitors live for their dogs, devoting time and money to their dogs' presentation, conditioning and training. Very few novices, even those with good dogs, will find themselves in the winners' circle, though it does happen. Don't be disheartened, though. Every exhibitor lifetime; it's certainly much better than a deer tick! Soon you will be envisioning yourself in the center ring at the Westminster Kennel Club Dog Show in New York City, competing for the prestigious Best in Show cup. This magical dog show is televised annually from Madison Square Garden, and the victorious dog becomes a celebrity overnight.

AKC CONFORMATION SHOWING

GETTING STARTED

Visiting a dog show as a spectator is a great place to start. Pick up the show catalog to find out what time your breed is being shown, who is judging the breed and in which ring the classes will be held. To start, Greater Swiss Mountain Dogs compete against other Greater Swiss Mountain Dogs, and the winner is selected as Best of Breed by the judge. This is the procedure for each breed. At a group

show, all of the Best of Breed winners go on to compete for Group One in their respective groups. For example, all Best of Breed winners in a given group compete against each other; this is done for all seven groups. Finally, all seven group winners go head to head in the ring for the Best in Show award.

What most spectators don't understand is the basic idea of conformation. A dog show is often referred as a "conformation" show. This means that the judge should decide how each dog stacks up (conforms) to the breed standard for his given breed: how well does this GSMD conform to the ideal representa-

Ch. Land's End Aunt Emily Fay winning Best of Breed at the South Windsor Kennel Club.

tive detailed in the standard? Ideally, this is what happens. In reality, however, this ideal often gets slighted as the judge compares Swissy #1 to Swissy #2. Again, the ideal is that each dog is judged based on his merits in comparison to his breed standard, not in comparison to the other dogs in the ring. It is easier for judges to compare dogs of the same breed to decide which they think is the better specimen; in the Group and Best in Show ring, however, it is very difficult to compare one breed to another, like apples to oranges. Thus the dog's conformation to the breed standard—not to mention advertising dollars and good handling—is essential to success in conformation shows. The dog described in the standard (the standard for each AKC breed is written and approved by the breed's national parent club and then submitted to the AKC for approval) is the perfect dog of that breed, and breeders keep their eye on the standard when they choose which dogs to breed, hoping to get closer and closer to the ideal with each litter.

Another good first step for the novice is to join a dog club. You will be astonished by the many and different kinds of dog clubs in the country, with about 5,000 clubs holding events every year. Most clubs require that prospective new members present two letters of recommendation from existing members. Perhaps you've made some friends visiting a show held by a particular club and you would like to join that club. Dog clubs may specialize in a

Having a successful day at the 2005 national specialty are Ch. Vulpecula of Bluegrass, Ch. Land's End Dinah and Ch. Land's End Nan's In Seattle.

FIRST
BROOD BITCH
NATIONAL SPECIALTY
GREATER SWISS
MOUNTAIN DOG
Club of America, Inc.

Littermates Ch. Barton Manor's Talla Lassie and Ch. Barton Manor's Teachers Pet, looking good at the Trenton Kennel Club.

single breed, like a local or regional Greater Swiss Mountain Dog club, or in a specific pursuit, such as obedience, draft-dog work or weight-pulling events. There are all-breed clubs for all dog enthusiasts; they sponsor special training days, seminars on topics like grooming or handling or lectures on breeding or canine genetics. There are also clubs that specialize in certain types of dogs, like herding dogs, working dogs, companion dogs, draft dogs, etc.

A parent club is the national organization, sanctioned by the AKC, which promotes and safeguards its breed in the country. The Greater Swiss Mountain Dog Club of America was formed in 1968 and can be contacted on the Internet at www.gsmdca.org. The parent club holds an annual national specialty show, usually in a different city each year, in which many of the country's top dogs, handlers and breeders gather to compete. At a specialty show, only members of a single breed are invited to participate. There are also group specialties, in which all members of a group are invited. For more information about dog clubs in your area, contact the AKC at www.akc.org on the Internet or write them at their Raleigh, NC address.

HOW SHOWS ARE ORGANIZED

Three kinds of conformation shows are offered by the AKC. There is the all-breed show, in which all AKC-recognized breeds can compete; the specialty show, which is for one breed only and usually sponsored by the breed's parent club; and the group show, for all breeds in one of the AKC's seven groups. The Greater Swiss Mountain Dog competes in the Working Group.

For a dog to become an AKC champion of record, the dog must earn 15 points at shows. The points must be awarded by at least three different judges and must include two "majors" under different judges. A "major" is a three-, four- or five-point win, and the number of points per win is determined by the number of dogs competing in the show on that day. (Dogs that are absent or are excused are not counted.) The number of points that are awarded varies from breed to breed. More dogs are needed to attain a major in more popular breeds, and fewer dogs are needed in less popular breeds. Yearly, the AKC evaluates the number of dogs in competition in each division (there are 14 divisions in all, based on geography) and may or may not change the numbers of dogs required for each number of points. For example, a major

in Division 2 (Delaware, New Jersey and Pennsylvania) recently required 17 dogs or 16 bitches for a three-point major, 29 dogs or 27 bitches for a four-point major and 51 dogs or 46 bitches for a five-point major. The Swissy attracts numerically proportionate representation at all-breed shows.

Only one dog and one bitch of each breed win points at a given show. There are no "co-ed" classes except for champions of record. Dogs and bitches do not compete against each other until they are champions. Dogs that are not champions (referred to as "class dogs") compete in one of five classes. The class in which a dog is entered depends on age and previous show wins. First there is the Puppy Class (sometimes divided further into classes for 6- to 12-month-olds and 12- to 18-month-olds); next is the Novice Class (for dogs that have no points toward their championship and whose only first-place wins have come in the Puppy Class or the Novice Class, the latter class limited to three first places); then there is the American-bred Class (for dogs bred in the US); the Bred-by-Exhibitor Class (for dogs handled by their breeders or by immediate family members of their breeders); and the Open Class (for any non-champions). Any dog may enter the Open

Class, regardless of age or win history, but to be competitive the dog should be older and have ring experience.

Ch. Barton Manor's Brooke winning Best of Breed at the Brookhaven Kennel Club.

The judge at the show begins judging the male dogs in the Puppy Class(es) and proceeds through the other classes. The judge awards first through fourth place in each class. The first-place winners of each class then compete with one another in the Winners Class to determine Winners Dog. The judge then starts over with the bitches, beginning with the Puppy Class(es) and proceeding up to the Winners Class to award Winners Bitch, just as he did with the dogs. A Reserve Winners Dog and Reserve Winners Bitch are also selected; they could be awarded the points in the case of a disqualification.

The Winners Dog and Winners Bitch are the two that are awarded the points for their breed. They then go on to compete with any champions of record (often called "specials") of their breed that are entered in the show. The champions may be dogs or bitches; in this class, all are shown together. The judge reviews the Winners Dog and Winners Bitch along with all of the champions to select the Best of Breed winner. The Best of Winners is selected between the Winners Dog and Winners Bitch; if one of these two is selected Best of Breed as well, he or she is automatically determined Best of Winners. Lastly, the judge selects Best of Opposite Sex to the Best of Breed winner. The Best of Breed winner then goes on to group competition.

At a group or all-breed show,

the Best of Breed winners from each breed are divided into their respective groups to compete against one another for Group One through Group Four. Group One (first place) is awarded to the dog that best lives up to the ideal for his breed as described in the standard. A group judge, therefore, must have a thorough working knowledge of many breed standards. After placements have been made in each group, the seven Group One winners (from the Sporting Group, Working Group, Hound Group, etc.) compete against each other for the top honor, Best in Show.

There are different ways to find out about dog shows in your area. The American Kennel Club's monthly magazine, the *American Kennel Gazette,* is accompanied by the *Events Calendar;* this magazine is available through subscription. You can also look on the AKC's and your parent club's websites for information and check the event listings in your local newspaper.

Your Greater Swiss Mountain Dog must be six months of age or older and registered with the AKC in order to be entered in AKC-sanctioned shows in which there are classes for the breed. Your Swissy also must not possess any disqualifying faults and must be

sexually intact. The reason for the latter is simple: dog shows are the proving grounds to determine which dogs and bitches are worthy of being bred. If they cannot be bred, that defeats the purpose! On that note, only dogs that have achieved championships, thus proving their excellent quality, should be bred. If you have spayed or neutered your dog, however, there are many AKC events other than conformation, such as obedience trials, agility trials and the Canine Good Citizen® Program, in which you and your Greater Swiss Mountain Dog can participate.

YOU'RE AT THE SHOW, NOW WHAT?
You will fill out an entry form when you register for the show. You must decide and designate on the form in which class you will enter your puppy or adult dog. Remember that some classes are more competitive than others and have limitations based on age and win history. Hopefully you will not be in the first class of the day, so you can take some time watching exactly how the judge is conducting the ring. Notice how the handlers are stacking their dogs, meaning setting them up. Does the judge prefer the dogs to be facing one direction or another? Take special note as to how the judge is moving the dogs and how he

is instructing the handlers. Is he moving them up and back, once or twice around, in a triangle?

If possible, you will want to get your number beforehand. Your assigned number must be attached as an armband on your outer garment. Do not enter the ring without your number. The ring steward will usually call the exhibits in numerical order. If the exhibits are not called in order, you should strategically place your dog in the line. For instance, if your pup is small for his age, don't stand him next to a large entry; if your dog is reluctant to gait, get at the end of the line-up so that you don't interfere with the other dogs. The judge's first direction, usually, is for all of the handlers to "take the dogs around," which means that everyone gaits his dog around the periphery of the ring.

While you're in the ring, don't let yourself (or your dog) become distracted. Concentrate on your dog; he should have your full attention. Stack him in the best way possible. Teach him to free-stand while you hold a treat out for him. Let him understand that he must hold this position for at least a minute before you reward him. Follow the judge's instruc-

Just another day at the show! The hustle and bustle, the other dogs and crowds of people become part of the routine to seasoned show dogs and exhibitors.

tions and be aware of what the judge is doing. Don't frustrate the judge by not paying attention to his directions.

When your dog's turn to be judged arrives, keep him steady and calm. The judge will inspect the dog's bite and dentition, overall musculature and structure and, in a male dog, the testicles, which must completely descend into the scrotum. Likewise, the judge will take note of the dog's alertness and temperament.

Aggressiveness is a disqualification in most breeds, and so is shyness. A dog must always be approachable by the judge, even if aloofness is one of the breed's characteristics. Once the judge has completed his hands-on inspection, he will instruct you to gait the dog. A dog's gait indicates to the judge that the dog is correctly constructed. Each breed standard describes the ideal correct gait for that breed. After the judge has inspected all of the dogs in the

Ch. Land's End Aunt Emily Fay continuing her winning ways at the 2005 Westminster Kennel Club Dog Show.

class in this manner, he will ask the entire class to gait together. He will make his final selections after one last look over the class.

Whether you win or lose, the only one disappointed will be you. Never let your dog know that he's not "the winner." Most important is that you reaffirm your dog's love of the game. Reward him for behaving properly and for being the handsome boy or pretty girl that he or she is.

After your first or second experience in the ring, you will know what things you need to work on. Go home, practice and have fun with your Swissy. With some time and effort, you and your well-trained show dog will soon be standing in the winners' circle with a blue ribbon!

OTHER TYPES OF COMPETITION

In addition to conformation shows, the AKC holds a variety of other competitive events. Obedience trials, agility trials and tracking trials are open to all breeds, while other events are limited to specific breeds or groups of breeds. The Junior Showmanship program is offered to aspiring young handlers and their dogs, and the Canine Good Citizen® Program is an all-around good-behavior test open to all dogs, pure-bred and mixed. The AKC does not sponsor draft-dog competition,

UKC WEIGHT PULLING

The United Kennel Club (UKC) is America's second oldest and second largest all-breed dog registry. The UKC sponsors conformation shows as well as an array of performance events to encourage the idea of the "total dog" that the club espouses. In addition to weight-pulling events sponsored by the GSMDCA, the Swissy can compete in UKC weight-pulling. Of course, not all breeds are talented or willing weight pullers, but many Swissys are. Basically, a dog is placed in a harness that is attached to a weighted vehicle, which the dog pulls a prescribed distance. The weighted vehicles operate either on wheels, on snow or on a rail system. The dogs are scored on how much weight they can pull; these scores are based on the proportion of the dog's body weight to the amount of weight pulled. Weight pulling requires quite a bit of training, with an emphasis on the dog's safety. The most important equipment required for weight pulling is a properly fitting harness. Once the handler has dropped the harness or traces (which connect the harness to the weighted vehicle), the dog is on his own. The handler can neither bait nor call the dog, and cannot touch the dog until he has crossed the finish line and the judge has signaled a "pull."

but the GSMDCA offers it and other ability contests.

OBEDIENCE TRIALS

Mrs. Helen Whitehouse Walker, a Standard Poodle fancier, can be credited with introducing obedience trials to the United States. In the 1930s she designed a series of exercises based on those of the Associated Sheep, Police, Army Dog Society of Great Britain. These exercises were intended to evaluate the working relationship between dog and owner. Since those early days of the sport in the US, obedience trials have grown more and more popular, and now more than 2,000 trials each year attract over 100,000 dogs and their owners. Any dog registered with the AKC, regardless of neutering or other disqualifications that would preclude entry in conformation competition, can participate in obedience trials.

There are three levels of difficulty in obedience competition. The first (and easiest) level is the Novice, in which dogs can earn the Companion Dog (CD) title. The intermediate level is the Open level, in which the Companion Dog Excellent (CDX) title is awarded. The advanced level is the Utility level, in which dogs compete for the Utility Dog (UD) title. Classes at each level are further divided into "A" and "B," with "A" for beginners and "B" for those with more experience. In order to win a title at a given level, a dog must earn three "legs." A "leg" is accomplished when a dog scores 170 or higher (200 is a perfect score). The scoring system gets a little trickier when you understand that a dog must score more than 50% of the points available for each exercise in order to actually earn the points. Available points for each exercise range between 20 and 40.

A dog must complete different exercises at each level of obedience. The Novice exercises are the easiest, with the Open and finally the Utility levels progressing in difficulty. Examples of Novice exercises are on- and off-lead heeling, a figure-8 pattern, performing a recall (or come), long sit and long down and standing for examination. In the Open level, the Novice-level exercises are required again, but this time without a leash and for longer durations. In addition, the dog must clear a broad jump, retrieve over a jump and drop on recall. In the Utility level, the exercises are quite difficult, including executing basic commands based on hand signals, following a complex heeling pattern, locating articles based on scent discrimination and completing jumps at the handler's direction.

Once he's earned the UD title, a dog can go on to win the prestigious title of Utility Dog Excellent (UDX) by winning "legs" in ten shows. Additionally, Utility Dogs who win "legs" in Open B and Utility B earn points toward the lofty title of Obedience Trial Champion (OTCh.). Established in 1977 by the AKC, this title requires a dog to earn 100 points as well as three first places in a combination of Open B and Utility B classes under three different judges. The "brass ring" of obedience competition is the AKC's National Obedience Invitational. This is an exclusive competition for only the cream of the obedience crop. In order to qualify for the invitational, a dog must be ranked in either the top 25 all-breeds in obedience or in the top 3 for his breed in obedience. The title at stake here is that of National Obedience Champion (NOC).

Barton Manor's Black Jack working on his first leg of an obedience title.

AGILITY TRIALS

Agility trials became sanctioned by the AKC in August 1994,

when the first licensed agility trials were held. Since that time, agility certainly has grown in popularity by leaps and bounds, literally! The AKC allows all registered breeds (including Miscellaneous Class breeds) to participate, providing the dog is 12 months of age or older, although the Swissy should not begin agility training until perhaps two years of age. Agility is designed so that the handler one eye and ear on the handler and the rest of his body on the course. The handler runs along with the dog, giving verbal and hand signals to guide the dog through the course.

The first organization to promote agility trials in the US was the United States Dog Agility Association, Inc. (USDAA). Established in 1986, the USDAA sparked the formation of many member clubs around the country. To participate in USDAA trials, dogs must be at least 18 months of age.

The USDAA and AKC both offer titles to winning dogs, although the exercises and requirements of the two organizations differ. Agility Dog (AD), Advanced Agility Dog (AAD) and Master Agility Dog (MAD) are the titles offered by the USDAA, while the AKC offers Novice Agility (NA), Open Agility (OA), Agility Excellent (AX) and Master Agility Excellent (MX). Beyond these four AKC titles, dogs can win additional titles in "jumper" classes: Jumper with Weave Novice (NAJ), Open (OAJ) and Excellent (MXJ). The ultimate title in AKC agility is MACH, Master Agility Champion. Dogs can continue to add number designations to the MACH title, indicating how many times the dog has met the title's requirements (MACH1, MACH2 and so on).

Ch. Barton MNRS Teachers Pet takes another title. demonstrates how well the dog can work at his side. The handler directs his dog through, over, under and around an obstacle course that includes jumps, tires, the dog walk, weave poles, pipe tunnels, collapsed tunnels and more. While working his way through the course, the dog must keep

Agility trials are a great way to keep your dog active, and they will keep you running, too! You should join a local agility club to learn more about the sport. These clubs offer sessions in which you can introduce your dog to the various obstacles as well as training classes to prepare him for competition. In no time, your dog will be climbing A-frames, crossing the dog walk and flying over hurdles, all with you right beside him. Your heart will leap every time your dog jumps through the hoop—and you'll be having just as much (if not more) fun!

TRACKING

Tracking tests are exciting ways to test your GSMD's instinctive scenting ability on a competitive level. All dogs have a nose, and all breeds are welcome in tracking tests. The first AKC-licensed tracking test took place in 1937 as part of the Utility level at an obedience trial, and thus competitive tracking was officially begun. The first title, Tracking Dog (TD), was offered in 1947, ten years after the first official tracking test. It was not until 1980 that the AKC added the title Tracking Dog Excellent (TDX), which was followed by the title Variable Surface Tracking (VST) in 1995. Champion Tracker (CT) is

GSMDCA EVENTS
At this time, the AKC does not sponsor breed-specific competitive events for the Swissy, but the GSMDCA offers competition and titles for drafting, herding, pack hiking, weight pulling and versatility. All of these events develop and test a Swissy's natural skills and instinctive abilities. For more detailed information about each event and to find out how to get involved with your Swissy, visit www.gsmdca.org and click on "Activities." There you also can learn more about getting into therapy work and search and rescue work with your Swissy.

awarded to a dog who has earned all three of those titles.

The TD level is the first and most basic level in tracking, progressing in difficulty to the TDX and then the VST. A dog must follow a track laid by a human 30 to 120 minutes prior in order to earn the TD title. The track is about 500 yards long and contains up to 5 directional changes. At the next level, the TDX, the dog must follow a 3- to 5-hour-old track over a course that is up to 1,000 yards long and has up to 7 directional changes. In the most difficult level, the VST, the track is up to 5 hours old and located in an urban setting.

INDEX

My Greater Swiss Mountain Dog

PUT YOUR PUPPY'S FIRST PICTURE HERE

Dog's Name _____

Date _____ Photographer _____